D0498374

NO LONGER PROPERTY OF
SEATTLE PUBLIC LIBRARY

Praise for *The Competitive Buddha*

"Yes, the Buddha does speak to sports, as illustrated in the distinguished career of Jerry Lynch. Who would think that like Jerry, the Buddha 'built' teams? If you doubt it, then read *The Competitive Buddha*—it will capture your imagination and enlighten your mind. This is joyful reading at its best."

> —Ron Adams, three-time assistant coach of the year for the World Champion NBA Golden State Warriors

"No other person has had more influence on my thirty-six years of coaching than Jerry Lynch. Whenever I need wisdom, insight, or inspiration, I look to Dr. Lynch. His work with Buddhist thought as applied to sports never fails to address the truly essential elements of coaching with the heart, as demonstrated by his latest book, *The Competitive Buddha*."

> —Missy Foote, head women's lacrosse coach at Middlebury College with six NCAA national championships to her credit, a seven-time national coach of the year, and member of the 2012 USA Lacrosse Hall of Fame

"Our team culture has truly been reshaped and remolded with Jerry's Buddha wisdom and guidance. We all feel honored to have had him work so closely with our team here at Boston University Women's Field Hockey. Our personal growth as coaches from his work will continue to benefit the program going forward. We have really enjoyed working with Jerry and his unusual Buddhist sports approach to leadership and performance."

> —Sally Starr, head coach of Boston University Women's Field Hockey and winner of sixteen conference championships

"Many people don't, but I love pineapple on pizza. So often it is when apparently different ideas bump together that new insights emerge. Jerry Lynch's *The Competitive Buddha* does not disappoint in this regard. The Buddha and sports?! Well, it turns out that some of the biggest insights in sport psychology—the ideas and techniques that elite athletes routinely use to approach their peak performances—are Buddhist to their core. *The Competitive Buddha* is a worthy contributor to this literature. And as a bonus, adopting the ideas in this book will help coaches and athletes 'win' more, in the broadest sense of word."

—Jim Thompson, Positive Coaching Alliance founder and author
of *Elevating Your Game: Becoming a Triple-Impact Competitor*

"If you're looking to live with deep inner peace—and at the same time perform toward the upper reaches of your potential in highly stressful and competitive environments, this book is for you, written by a man who is considered by many to be an authority on the confluence of ancient philosophy, psychology, and sports."

—Michael Gervais, PhD, high performance psychologist and
host of the nationally acclaimed podcast *Finding Mastery*

"*The Competitive Buddha* affirms there is no path to mastery because mastery *is* the path, the path of the Warrior Mystic. Such a warrior is one who is fiercely committed to competing at the highest level, and at the same time, doing so in Love, Joy, Connection, Compassion, Collaboration, and Cooperation (the four Cs). Jerry is a warrior mystic, a competitive Buddha, and a kindred spirit committed to service, helping others to reach their full human potential."

—George Mumford, athlete, Zen Buddhist teacher,
and author of *The Mindful Athlete*

"In sports, we are often led to believe that competitiveness and joy cannot coexist. We are told that it is impossible to build a selfless team in a world of self-centeredness. We are told that love and compassion have no place in the cutthroat world of youth, college, and professional sports. We have been misled. In *The Competitive Buddha*, my great friend and mentor Dr. Jerry Lynch teaches us how the ideals of the Buddha—joy, compassion, selflessness, connection, and patience—bring balance to sport and will help you unleash the greatest version of yourself. It is a *must*-read for all my teams."

—John O'Sullivan, author of *Every Moment Matters* and
founder of the Changing the Game Project

"Jerry Lynch is a great teacher of mastery, expressed masterfully in this brilliant book. He shows how so many Buddhist values are critical to success in sports and life: Mindfulness and Presence, Selflessness and Patience, Gratitude and Compassion, Respect and Humility, and more. This book will rouse the Joy of Competition, teach you that The Path is the Goal, and inspire you to Never Give Up!"

—Dr. Joseph Parent, Buddhist teacher and author of *Zen Golf*

"What an incredible, must-read book from one of the best in the business of performance and leadership. The lessons, principles, and strategies that you will learn in this book from this master teacher are the same that Jerry used to help my University of Maryland Lacrosse team to win seven consecutive national championships. *The Competitive Buddha* is a book that will fill your craving for connection, caring, compassion, cooperation, and collaboration not just in the locker room, but in the boardroom as well. Brilliant stuff!"

—Cindy Timchal, eight-time national women's Lacrosse
championship winner as head coach at University of Maryland

"I count Jerry as a friend who has given me much encouragement. He has made a difference by helping me to lead, coach, inspire, and empower my athletes to reaching their potential. This is a good time for this book, *The Competitive Buddha*."

—Phil Jackson, head coach of NBA Championship
Bulls and Lakers and author of *Eleven Rings*

"Jerry Lynch is one of the few people who knows that the Buddha was the first student athlete, excelling both in the classroom (where he mastered sixty-four scripts) and outside, where he bested his opponents in archery, weight-lifting, and wrestling. In *The Competitive Buddha*, Jerry brings the insights of the Buddhist tradition back to the playing field, where they began so long ago."

—Donald Lopez, PhD, professor of Buddhist Studies
and author of *Buddha Takes the Mound*

"I was a philosophy major and an elite soccer athlete in college. It was always a challenge to understand how these two disciplines could converge. What I love about Jerry's work is how he effortlessly helps us to experience the relevancy of Buddhism to sports. In *The Competitive Buddha*, he imparts an abundance of time-honored, sacred wisdom and makes it easily accessible for immediate use, both for my athletes and my coaching and leadership. Jerry is a wise and trusted friend who has a very positive effect on me and my program at UNC."

—Anson Dorrance, head coach for women's soccer with twenty-
two national championships at the University of North Carolina

"I have known Jerry for over twenty years; we worked together at Duke, as well as more recently, with my career culminating now as head coach of the Utah Jazz. He has been a friend, a confidant, and a profound mentor with enormous influence on my leadership and coaching skill set over the years. Jerry's unique and innovative approach to athletics and life is unparalleled. His latest book, *The Competitive Buddha*, is arguably his best work of his forty-year career, and it will inspire you as it has me to continue your journey to be the best you can be in all aspects of sports and life. This is a remarkable book."

—Quin Snyder, head coach of the NBA Utah Jazz

"I think this is Jerry's best book yet, a book that jibes perfectly with my vision for the Warriors."

—Steve Kerr, head coach of the NBA Golden State Warriors

"I have been coaching golf for over thirty years, training some of the top golfers in the world including Patrick Reed, the 2018 PGA Masters Champion. To achieve this level in my work, I have leaned heavily on Jerry's books, especially his latest, *The Competitive Buddha*. This book contains all of the profound and pertinent wisdom that he has passed on to me, lessons I use daily with my athletes and myself. Jerry's teachings in *The Competitive Buddha* have altered how I perceive the world."

—Kevin Kirk, 2019 PGA Coach of the Year and
director of Golf Instruction at The Woodlands

"I have had the pleasure of knowing Jerry Lynch for over two decades now, have read all of his books, and have worked with him personally on my mental game of competition. He is amazing, and his books and counseling have not only helped me, but I have shared his principles with so many others. Jerry has a brilliant knack for relating the basic principles of Taoist and Buddhist thought to his success in coaching in a joyful, understandable way in his conference and books. His latest book, *The Competitive Buddha*, may be the best yet!"

—Barry Siff, ultra-endurance athlete, coach, event organizer, author, and Olympic sports leader over four decades, who served as the president of USA Triathlon, the CEO of USA Team Handball, and an advisor to USA Boxing

"My work with Jerry Lynch over the last eighteen years has transformed my competitive kayaking career as well as my life outside of sport. Not only has Jerry helped me achieve higher levels of competitive athletics, he has also empowered and inspired me as a doctor to use lessons from sport to help heal the patients in my Uganda medical clinic. In his latest book, *The Competitive Buddha*, Jerry offers the same essential wisdom and guidance he has taught me over the years to help me up my game and be the best version of myself and have fun doing it. This book is a game changer for anyone and everyone! I use its messages and lessons all the time."

—Jessie Stone, MD, CEO of Stone Medical Clinic in Uganda, five-time USA Women's Freestyle Kayak National Team member, and USA Women's Freestyle Kayak National Champion in 2020

"Dr. Lynch is very insightful and caring. His lessons are powerful and invaluable. You will definitely take away many gems from this book that will assist in your coaching and athletic goals."

—Mike Hawkes, director of athletics at Shining
Mountain High School, Boulder, Colorado

"I have been fortunate to achieve success at the highest levels in the sport of women's lacrosse, and I consider Jerry Lynch's teachings a huge part of that success. During my journey from being recognized with All-American honors at the University of North Carolina to being a three-time gold medalist on the National Team, Jerry made an incredible impact on me as a player. As a coach at Delaware, Stanford, Ohio State, and currently at Johns Hopkins University, my approach to coaching lacrosse is directly influenced by Jerry's teachings and his work. This book, *The Competitive Buddha*, gives insight into these teachings and how they have not only been applied by Jerry in the sports world, but how they are transferable to any line of endeavor. The culture developed through his work has helped teams of which I personally have been a part to reach incredible success. From his direct involvement in UNC's journey to the national championship in 2013 and 2016 and indirect influence in Team USA's gold medals in 2009, 2013, and 2017, it is obvious his teachings on la familia, joy, compassion, and competition encourage a mentality of being in the moment, which also instills confidence and trust within a team. I am extremely grateful for Jerry and his shared wisdom. After reading *The Competitive Buddha*, you too will be inspired and learn that mastery, leadership, and success in life are truly created when you win from within, open your heart, and give your best to others."

—Kristin Carr, three-time All-America lacrosse athlete
at the University of North Carolina, three-time world
champion on Team USA women's lacrosse, and associate
head lacrosse coach at Johns Hopkins University

"If anyone could possibly achieve this special feat of finding a perfect East/West synthesis, blending the Western Sport Mind with the Eastern Meditative Heart, it would be my old friend Dr. Jerry Lynch. Since our collaboration on the book, *Thinking Body, Dancing Mind*, I have marveled at Jerry's boundless searching mind in furthering his perpetual learning and sharing. His *The Competitive Buddha* is a brilliant book that has achieved a down-to-earth way to teach us the profound mystery of the Yin/Yang balance in our lives."

—Chungliang Al Huang, founder-president of the Living Tao Foundation, author of *Embrace Tiger* and *Return to Mountain*, and coauthor of *Tao: The Watercourse Way*

"Now more than ever, our coaches and athletes are starving for deeper authentic connections. Jerry's work has helped me and the student athletes in our program to be grounded in what makes for a truly transformational life experience through sport. Tapping more into the 'why we do' has elevated 'what we do' to new heights. His concepts in *The Competitive Buddha* have been instrumental in helping these youngsters to not simply win the game, but to win in their daily lives. The Buddha way has guided us to be champions on and off the pitch."

—Hardy Kalisher, NHSCA national high school boys' soccer coach of the year in 2017, two-time Colorado state champion, and five-time conference champion coach at Boulder High

"*The Competitive Buddha* is a pure expression of a new and refreshing, competitive yet servant-led *mind* space. This book will help you to pause, pivot, reset, rewire, and refire as we *seek* together and *win* where it really counts. Jerry is the master of this, and his book is a reflection of all the awesome Buddha work we did together with our storied program at the University of Maryland. Jerry demonstrates a warrior spirit with a teacher's heart, not just in his work, but in his personal life as well."

> —Missy Meharg, head coach of the University of Maryland's women's field hockey team, winner of seven NCAA national championships, twenty-six conference titles, and nine-time national coach of the year awards

"Opening your heart and mind to Jerry's teachings is truly transformational. If you seek excellence and mastery for yourself and those you lead, *The Competitive Buddha* is a must-read! The win-at-all-cost culture of Western sport has paralyzed the growth of the human spirit. In this extraordinary book, Jerry uses Buddhist insights to teach the balance between the physical and the spiritual, encouraging the interconnectedness needed to build transcendent teams and finding real joy in the harmonious dance of competitive sports. Once again, a brilliant teaching book for anyone who strives to up their game in athletics and life."

> —Jenny Levy, head coach for women's Lacrosse at University of North Carolina, winner of two NCAA national championships

"Dr. Jerry Lynch's latest endeavor to shed his brilliant illumination on the best of the competitive spirit is his most compelling yet! His storytelling is incredible and gives richness and meaning to the entire competitive journey. This special book comes at a time when unifying the human spirit around deeply grounded principles and values is more relevant and compelling than ever. He does so with grace, deep insight, and humility. Jerry's leadership and leadership advice has been deeply impactful in my professional and personal life and I am deeply grateful for his ongoing contribution in the competitive arena."

> —Bob Hansen, head men's tennis coach at Middlebury
> College, winner of eight NCAA national championships

"Combining insights from the worlds of sports and spirituality, *The Competitive Buddha* shows us the power of competing with, not against, each other. Jerry helps us to move beyond our fears to greater faith in ourselves and one another while focusing on the larger process in athletics and life. This is an important book for our time."

> —Diane Dreher, PhD, author of *The Tao of Personal
> Leadership* and associate director of Santa Clara
> University's Spirituality and Health Institute

"Dr. Jerry Lynch's new book, *The Competitive Buddha*, will allow us to add another thread to the fabric of our national championship culture at the University of Connecticut. Jerry's impact on our team has been immeasurable. Following the path of mindfulness and competing with a warrior's open heart has allowed our team to reach the pinnacle of our sport. Jerry is a gifted coach, teacher, and author who continues to inspire us through his work."

> —Nancy Stevens, head women's field hockey coach at the University of Connecticut and all-time winningest women's field hockey coach with three national championships and nineteen conference championships

"I am especially excited about Jerry Lynch's latest book *The Competitive Buddha* because my name, Tara, is a Buddhist deity known for compassion and action. In his book, Jerry describes how successful athletes and coaches are both competitive (action) and caring (compassion). As a coach, I work to teach basketball skills and encourage individual growth and teamwork while, like the Buddha, always bringing joy to the gym! Thank you, Jerry, for all the good work we did together and for writing this important book. It is right up my alley!"

> —Tara VanDerveer, women's head basketball coach at Stanford University (with three national and twenty-nine conference championships), Olympic Gold Medal head coach, and coach of the US women's national basketball team

"The writings of Dr. Jerry Lynch have informed and inspired me since the early days of my coaching career almost thirty years ago, and they sustain me in my leadership and work as an athletics director, as well as in my personal life. In *The Competitive Buddha*, Jerry once again combines ancient wisdom with practical, modern approaches to build better athletes, coaches, and leaders with lessons that are applicable both on the field of play and the game of life."

—Erin Quin, director of athletics, Middlebury College

"Jerry Lynch came into my life at just the right time, and his teachings and books have had a profound impact on me. Jerry continues to be a guiding force in my life, reminding me to follow my heart. From his first book, *Thinking Body, Dancing Mind*, to his most recent book, *The Competitive Buddha*, Jerry's words center me so I can think more clearly, be present in the moment, and lead free from distraction. *The Competitive Buddha* reaffirms the pertinent lessons I have learned from him over the past twenty-five years and reminds me how important they are to share with future leaders. Leading with love from your heart doesn't make you soft, it makes you stronger and more connected to those around you. In this book, Jerry gives examples of how to do this, and I know from experience it has helped me in my leadership and can help you in yours."

—Karen Henning, head women's lacrosse coach at Colby College
and winner of five national championships in Women's Lacrosse

"In his latest book, Jerry continues to explore dimensions of consciousness that will help you to view competition in a profound, refreshing way. In *The Competitive Buddha*, he transforms the world of athletics into a sacred space for absorbing practical, usable life lessons and ageless wisdom for higher performance, not just in sports but in all of life."

> —Michael Murphy, founder of Esalen Institute
> and author of *Golf in the Kingdom*

"I have been competing in tennis for the last thirty-seven years, traveling on a path toward just winning more. Reading many of Jerry Lynch's books, starting with his extraordinary eye-opener *Thinking Body, Dancing Mind*, has led me toward a new path of finding the wins within the win. *The Competitive Buddha* presents, with beauty and clarity, the ultimate goals of competition and high performance in every aspect of our lives. This book will change your life and your view of the world."

> —Bob Litwin, Former number-one senior tennis world
> champion, twenty-five-time US National Champion,
> and author of *Live the Best Story of Your Life*

"Jerry's new book *The Competitive Buddha* is truly a roadmap to a sound yet strong and precise mind. I love how the book takes a deep dive into how to focus on the right things in your life so that your athletic career can truly thrive. I learned how the Buddha is less focused on the outcomes of an event, choosing instead to attend to the journey of living in peace and becoming the best version of yourself. Adapting this Buddha mindset into my professional surfing career has made a massive positive impact."

> —Lakey Peterson, philanthropist, professional surfer who
> finished second and third in the world in 2018 and 2019,
> and winner of multiple World Championship tour events

"Sports psychologist Lynch (*Thinking Body, Dancing Mind*) uses Buddhist wisdom and inspirational anecdotes in this beneficial guide to improving one's competitive ability. For Lynch, competition is a 'natural state of collaboration, connection, compassion and cooperation,' and athletes who follow Buddhist teachings can detach from the ego and the need for praise to achieve calmness and clarity, live in the now by observing what is happening around them, and offer humility and praise for defeated opponents. Star athletes including Kobe Bryant, Derek Jeter, and Chris Wondolowski used meditation and relaxation techniques to focus on their game, Lynch writes, while coaches can take on the role of 'servant leader,' as seen by Golden State Warriors coach Steve Kerr's method of empowering his players to reach their full potential. Though the material can be repetitive, Lynch digs deep into the athlete's mindset and provides numerous examples of Buddhist wisdom in action. Athletes and coaches alike will find plenty of takeaways here."

—Publishers Weekly

The
Competitive
Buddha

*How To Up Your Game in Sports,
Leadership and Life*

More Books by Jerry Lynch

Thinking Body, Dancing Mind

Way of the Champion

Let Them Play

Win the Day

Coaching with Heart

Spirit of the Dancing Warrior

Tao Mentoring

Creative Coaching

Working Out Working Within

The
Competitive
Buddha

How to Up Your Game in Sports,

Leadership and Life

Jerry Lynch

Foreword by Steve Kerr, Head Coach of Golden State Warriors

Mango Publishing

CORAL GABLES

Copyright © 2021 by Jerry Lynch.
Published by Mango Publishing Group, a division of Mango Media Inc.

Cover Design: Roberto Nuñez
Cover Illustration: Olha Huro, Dreamstime.com
Layout & Design: Carmen Fortunato

Mango is an active supporter of authors' rights to free speech and artistic expression in their books. The purpose of copyright is to encourage authors to produce exceptional works that enrich our culture and our open society.

Uploading or distributing photos, scans or any content from this book without prior permission is theft of the author's intellectual property. Please honor the author's work as you would your own. Thank you in advance for respecting our author's rights.

For permission requests, please contact the publisher at:
Mango Publishing Group
2850 S Douglas Road, 2nd Floor
Coral Gables, FL 33134 USA
info@mango.bz

For special orders, quantity sales, course adoptions and corporate sales, please email the publisher at sales@mango.bz. For trade and wholesale sales, please contact Ingram Publisher Services at customer.service@ingramcontent.com or +1.800.509.4887.

The Competitive Buddha: How to Up Your Game in Sports, Leadership and Life

Library of Congress Cataloging-in-Publication number: 2021936317
ISBN: (print) 978-1-64250-589-4, (ebook) 978-1-64250-590-0
BISAC category code SPO066000, SPORTS & RECREATION / Cultural & Social Aspects

Printed in the United States of America

I dedicate this book to the late, great Kobe Bryant; with his diligent, intentional, fearlessly mindful Mamba Mentality, coupled with his daily meditation practice and desire to continually up his game and be the best version of himself, he was emblematic of the quintessential competitive Buddha in sports, leadership, and life.

Contents

FOREWORD

In 1992, early in my NBA playing career, I was lost. I was a marginal player in my fourth season, hanging onto my position with the Cleveland Cavaliers. I was good enough to make it in the NBA, but I couldn't get out of my own way. I needed to trust myself and my abilities—to let loose and really go for it. Instead, I found myself in a constant state of caution, in "don't make a mistake" mode, and my game suffered.

My best friend on the team, Danny Ferry, knew I was struggling, and he told me about a book he had been reading called *Thinking Body, Dancing Mind* by Jerry Lynch. Danny suggested that I read it as a way of finding the rhythm and flow that I was searching for. At the time, I really didn't know much about Eastern philosophy, so when I learned about Taoism and how it was really just a practical guide to a simple, clear way of living and being, I was intrigued. After all, my own mind was severely clouded with thoughts of failure in my career, and all I really wanted was to let myself play without interference.

Thinking Body, Dancing Mind became a crucial element in my development that year as an athlete and as a person. The book was filled not only with Taoist wisdom, but with practical techniques that I was able to apply to my training on the basketball court every day. With this new approach to my career, I was able to break through that season with one of the best stretches of my career. I started the final fifteen games or so for a very good Cleveland team, and I felt freer than I had ever felt on the court. In fact, the basket never looked so big to me in my entire life! Raising my level of play so dramatically helped to increase my stock around the league, and I went on to play another eleven seasons in the NBA.

Just as importantly, reading Jerry's book—and later meeting him—changed the way I thought about sports and life in general. I began to realize how much power existed in the delicate balance between the mind and the body. Playing for the Bulls was where I ultimately felt that intersection most strongly, because while Michael Jordan brought an almost maniacal physical competitiveness to the gym every day, Phil Jackson brought a sense of calm and mindfulness. This beautiful balance served as the foundation of those championship Bulls teams; and as my worlds and thoughts continued to collide, it was not a surprise to find that Jerry Lynch and Phil Jackson were friends who shared a deep connection through this evolved yet ancient way of thinking and being. Through Phil, Jerry and I began our own friendship—one that has lasted for more than twenty-five years. During our trips to the West Coast every season, I would see Jerry and his family and we would catch up on his latest books, my family and career happenings, and everything in between.

The decades have passed and times have changed, but Jerry and I have remained in touch, and ironically, we are now both in the business of helping people find the best versions of themselves. For me, what began as a lesson in new ways of thinking about playing and competing back in my early twenties has evolved in my mid-fifties into a full philosophy of coaching. Having been blessed with the amazing opportunity to lead the Golden State Warriors the past six seasons, my staff and I have instituted a core philosophy that is built on finding the balance between competition and joy. Jerry, meanwhile, has written a book that jives perfectly with my vision for the Warriors, *The Competitive Buddha*. The book lays out Jerry's quest to use sports to teach Buddhist values like connection, selflessness, compassion, patience, and love, and *then* goes on to reveal how Buddhist wisdom can foster healthy, competitive, masterful performance environments in sports, business, and life. I think this is Jerry's best book yet, and it's not by accident. Jerry is a lifelong learner—which I also aspire to be—and a lifetime of living and learning has led to his beautiful work about Buddha for better sports and sports for learning the way of the Buddha—a two-way street that is ultimately about helping people find joy and contentment in their craft and in their life.

Enjoy your journey, continue learning and seeking knowledge, and find wisdom and contentment as you travel down your own path. Peace.

STEVE KERR

PREFACE

The beautiful, attractive Japanese brush stroke calligraphy art that adorns the cover of this book is the *enso* circle, originating in Japan hundreds of years ago. It is emblematic of the Zen Buddhist culture and the Japanese refer to it simply as *enso*, as the word *enso* (pronounced en'—so or en'—zo) by itself refers to a circle. Its simplicity yet profoundness is its ultimate sophistication.

I believe that this sacred iconic symbol is perhaps more relevant today than ever. It represents enlightenment, great strength, elegance, oneness, harmony, cooperation, collaboration, connection, unity, cohesion, emptiness, and the infinite circular journey of life. Its letter O shape is symbolic of oneness of heart and soul; its empty center reminds us that to learn and grow, our minds must remain empty so we can fill ourselves up with new wisdom. The circle is also representative of transformative power, "power with," the "power to," and "power from within," *not* merely transactional "power over." Notice when you are standing in a circle that nobody is above or under you and no one is in front or in back of you, symbolic of the type of power inherent in service, diversity, and equity.

I chose the dual colors of red and black because they take on special meaning with respect to the book's message. The color black in this case represents power, strength, sophistication, boldness, and elegance. Red, on the other hand, is symbolic of heart, love, passion, change, transformation, and fire. Anything that comes in contact with fire changes or transforms. These two colors together are emblematic of the messages learned in this book, a book about change, transformation, personal power, boldness, passion, and love as you take this infinite journey of upping your game in sports, leadership, and life.

I want you to know that I use this concept in my work all the time with my championship teams over the last thirty plus years. The *circle* is a reference point and a reminder of who we are, what we do, and most importantly, why we do it. The significance of the circle is particularly germane to sports when you think about it. All balls are round: A home run is referred to as a round-tripper—you round the bases; you play a round of golf, placing the ball in a round circular hole. Basketball is often called a game of hoops or round ball, and you circle the bases in baseball; the circle appears in center court and on the midfield line, and defenses and offenses mimic circular patterns. There are extensive examples.

I introduce my teams to this powerful concept from the very moment that we meet in a circle, and I ask the players to conduct their practices and games from that sacred space and go outward from there. When we assemble in the circle for the first time, I briefly remind them of its significance for our culture, what I want them to take from it, and how to apply this understanding to the team's journey. Here is what I talk about with them, and I encourage you to do the same when introducing this cross-cultural symbol to your group or team.

- As we stand in this circle, notice how we stand together side by side, unified as one, connected and cohesive.

- Notice that the circle represents the universal, divine mystical journey with no ending.

- The center of the circle is an empty space. Let it be a reminder of how we can keep our minds empty, full of potential, and ready to be filled with all that we need to know as we go forward, leading us to be open and receptive to new possibilities. In Japanese, this "negative space" is called *ma*, an idea that reminds us to step back and see with a whole perspective. It expresses the concept of "less is more" in one word.

- The shape of the circle is the letter "O," which stands for our *oneness* of heart and *oneness* of soul: one mission, one goal. Feel connected with our hearts.

- When we form this shape as we gather, it allows us to see each other eye to eye; the eyes as the windows to the soul nonverbally communicate our readiness to serve one another and go to battle for something bigger than individual conflicts with each other.

- Notice how we are all equal in the circle…There is no one in front of you, no one in back, no one above you, and no one below. We are equal yet diverse, whole and inclusive, connected and strong.

- We are a protected boundary, not to be penetrated by the opponent or made unwelcome.

- With your eyes closed, feel the energy and strength of our group. Remember your promises to go out and win the day.

At first, you may have to read the lines above to the group until they are memorized. But either way, the power of the circle is felt by all. Every time the team enters the circle— whether before the start of practice, prior to a game, or during team locker room meetings or bonding and team building exercises—the athletes can feel such power. I always use the circle as the starting point of any team activity that signals…we are ready to begin.

INTRODUCTION

COMPETITIVENESS THE BUDDHA WAY

By now you are probably saying, 'What? Wait! The Buddha is competitive? Isn't that an oxymoron? Why would the author choose a provocative title like *The Competitive Buddha?*' Let me clarify and shed some light on this. Though it is not well-known, it is widely accepted by those familiar with Buddhist teachings that the Buddha could have been the original competitive athlete. The presence of Buddhism in sport is best exemplified by boxing and wrestling, both of which played a big part in monastic life. These athletes were blessed by monks prior to competition, a cultural phenomenon distinct from the traditional Buddhist way. It appears that the relationship between the Buddha and competitive sports is not what many believe it to be.

During his youth, the Buddha practiced body-focused yoga in his quest for enlightenment. He also was an avid competitive wrestler, a great archer, and a gallant horseman. Through these strenuous activities and competitive sports, he learned spiritual lessons about commitment, discipline, cooperation, collaboration, connectedness, compassion, persistence, and sacrifice as he became an indomitable spirit with a strong lifelong work ethic. This competitive Buddha way was revolutionary even by most of today's standards and is more important now than ever. His opponents were his partners on a journey of assisting each other to aspire to the achievement of mastery, the essence of the competitive Buddha.

Part of the mission of this book is to debunk the classic myth that competition is bad and contrary to the values of the Buddha. Competition can have negative implications in Buddhist terms when you desire victory at any cost, even if it means hurting or being unkind to others.

For the Buddha, healthy competition occurs when your focus is on developing your skills and you refuse to have bad feelings if another wins. True competition is not about winning or losing. According to the Buddha, "Giving up winning or losing, one lives in peace and happiness." This is what the Buddha calls the cultivation of *mudita*, being joyful and happy for the good fortune of others. In Latin, the word for competition is *competere*, "to seek or strive together" to reach one's greatness. According to Buddhist thought, "If you light a lantern for another, it will also brighten your path."

These brilliant words refer to competition as a natural state of collaboration, connection, compassion, and cooperation. Life and sports are more fun when we experience the power of these C's and compete *with* rather than *against* another. When we do so, we help each other to discover aspects of self we never knew existed. True competition in the Buddha sense is about interconnectedness and striving together to become part of something greater than ourselves. Your success, like the Buddhist idea of success, is the result of being aligned with this notion. In fact, this speaks to the collective consciousness of all who enter into the harmonious dance of competitive sports. For example, I have marinated the nervous systems of members of all my 115 championship teams in this philosophy, and I want to say that the competitive Buddha teams that demonstrate compassion, cooperation, connection, and collaboration exude love, passion, fearlessness, and loyalty to each other. Winning is the natural by-product of *The Competitive Buddha*'s approach.

In his classic bestseller *Outliers: The Story of Success*, Malcolm Gladwell makes it perfectly clear that "No one, not rock stars, not pro athletes, not software billionaires and not even geniuses, ever makes it alone." Working together, the competitive Buddha edge is a calling to help each other person to become a better version of themself through competition.

I remember adapting this competitive approach during my athletic career as an elite distance runner; while winning a national championship, I was bathed in this competitive Buddha way. For example, my opponents were not my enemies who needed to be defeated. They were helpful partners who would bring out my best. If they passed me on a hill, I'd respond with a surge that helped me realize I had more left "in the tank." Using this Buddha method, I was less anxious, less worried, felt safer, and had more fun reaching that better version of myself.

Competitive Buddha sports is an opportunity to view competition in a refreshing new way. It helps you to work hard, to be present, and to respect those with whom you compete. The question you must ask is: Am I striving to be better than my opponent or to improve upon my previous self? Look at competition as a natural way of helping each other to raise our collective levels of performance in sports, business, and life by giving and receiving with an open heart—an experiential alternative for all competitive arenas. Perhaps we need to consider a shift from a fierce "win at all costs" way of being competitive to a more fulfilling, meaningful approach.

What to Take from This Book

The Competitive Buddha is about the humanistic side of competing and coaching—it's about connection, cooperation, compassion, collaboration, and a more mindful way of mastering our craft. In this book, I work diligently to bring carefully chosen spiritual laws, principles, and strategies of Buddhist thought into the world of sports. By doing this, I hope that you will be able to heighten your joy and happiness while reducing the suffering in your life. Sport is one of the few activities in life that can help you to do this. As a lifelong student of philosophy, psychology, and athletics, I have learned that doing so is possible, and I want this book to help you to experience a sea change, or fundamental shift, in your level of performance.

This book is about mastery, leadership, and spirituality. Reading it, you will learn what you need to keep, what you need to discard, and what you need to add to your mental, emotional, and spiritual skill set as an athlete, coach, leader, parent, CEO, or in any other field in life where you want to perform your best. You will learn not only about how Buddhism can help you to be better prepared for sports and life, but how sports and life can teach you about Buddhism. You will discover how people from all parts of the world have brought together the Buddha and athletics for greater fun, enjoyment, and pleasure during their athletic efforts. I will demonstrate how certain timeless core Buddha values will inspire you to embrace and navigate the unchartered waters of mastery. I believe you will find the Buddha mind and the Kobe Bryant Mamba Mentality both quite interesting and very useful.

When it comes to leadership and coaching, this book will teach you how the best of the best coaches today use these ancient methods for our modern times, especially when it comes to the *servant leader* concept. You will learn very specific strategies and techniques to implement this special way to guide and lead.

All of this is supplemented with inspiring Zen stories as well as an extensive bibliography to help you continue to learn and use these teachings for a lifetime.

New Buddhism for the West

The teachings of Buddha are not about a doctrine or speculation. The teachings are about what is true. This book gives you the chance to master Buddha truth through athletics while simultaneously mastering sports through Buddha truth. It's a simple yet powerful back-and-forth dance between the physical and the spiritual.

Throughout this book, you will discover natural laws, precepts, principles, and other helpful and appropriate ways to reduce the suffering felt when things don't turn out the way you'd like...as in loss, defeat, attachment to winning, and other challenges inherent in the arena of athletics. *The Competitive Buddha* is a book about truth; that is, it's about the way things are meant to be as opposed to the way we think they should be. When this competitive Buddha way is embraced, you are on the path of mastery, not the path to mastery. This is a subtle nuance that makes all the difference in every type of performance, in or out of the arena of sports.

The concept of the competitive Buddha has evolved for me over the years. I have adopted and adapted it in a more Western way during all my work with athletes, coaches, and teams, using the teaching and wisdom of the Buddha to help them to discover and embrace a simpler yet more powerful way to mastery, leadership, and spiritual evolution, as well as taking their game in both sports and life to higher levels, of performance.

This book will be your guide on this joyful path. In it, I combine ancient Buddhist thought with Western psychology to help you experience effort without effort—to win from within as you mind the heart and mend the mind. For the purposes of this book, it's important to know that Buddhism is used here not as a dogma or religion; rather, it is a practical way of understanding experience based on the Four Noble Truths and the Noble Eightfold Path of Buddhist thought.

I do not intend to tell you what to believe in. I do hope to show you what to think—or perhaps, what not to think. The Westernized version of Buddhism is very simple in nature and will enable you to take on only that which is relevant in your sport and life. This refreshing approach, which applies core Buddhist insights to our modern times, is often referred to as the "New Buddhism for the West," as it influences Western culture in the arts, in social activism, and in athletics.

I am aware that there are many Buddhist traditions, but in this book, I humbly select a fundamental core of ideas to focus on which are found in most of these traditions, avoiding getting into the more deeply esoteric parts of Buddhist philosophy and psychology. I'm not trying to help all of us to become better Buddhists. I simply want us to be better versions of ourselves.

Following this clarifying introduction to set the competitive Buddha sports table, I have divided this book into four distinct parts. They represent the four seasons of the year, beginning with Spring in Part One. The four parts complete one full cycle representing the Buddhist Enso circle as it appears on the cover: The circle is the endless Buddha sports journey, open yet complete.

Part One, "When Buddha and Sports Converge," portrays the vast, diversified population of athletes who rely on the teaching of the Buddha for leadership, mastery, and spirituality in their sport and life. Making these profound connections serves as a demonstration of how Buddhism is used globally in conjunction with sports. In this section, you will see convincing evidence of the potential usefulness and importance of such teachings in your particular athletic endeavor and life as well.

In Part Two, "Buddha Brain, Mamba Mind," you will begin to understand the intimate connection between the Buddhist mindset and the mentality of Kobe Bryant as I introduce a plethora of mental and spiritual guides and truths for helping you to create significant change in performance. The Mamba Mind and the Competitive Buddha are intricately entwined.

In Part Three, "Noble Mindful Leadership," you will be introduced to the path of effective Buddha leadership and how to become a mindful coach with an open heart via the practice of meditation as you cultivate love and compassion for others. Also, I will help you to understand the intimate relationship between the Noble Eightfold Path and the specific qualities and traits of a mindful Buddha.

In Part Four, "The Sound of One Hand Clapping," I offer thirty-two Zen Buddhist stories and parables that will inspire and empower you in very insightful ways and illuminate your path of mastery. Storytelling, as we all know, is one of the most provocative and profound methods of absorbing new learnings.

Finally, I have included an invaluable epilogue called "From Little Streams Come Big Rivers" and a rich bibliography of the essential classics I used to help me gather my thoughts on this subject as well as others I have found helpful in guiding me to stay on the competitive Buddha path.

The Hole in the Flute

This book is not just for those in athletics but for anyone interested in the potential of the human spirit. I simply use the arena of athletics as a vehicle to explore leadership and masterful performance in sports and all arenas of life. In his classic tome *Golf in the Kingdom*, Michael Murphy talks about developing "astronauts of inner space" who break through to levels of awareness not yet explored by the human race. I hope to scratch the surface of his concept and help all of us be such explorers.

My book is not an impeccable masterpiece on Buddhist thought. Writing this book was a daunting task. I was overwhelmed at times because there is so much to comprehend, so much to know. So, I decided to stick to basic simple truths that I can wrap my head around. I don't claim to know much, but what I do know, I will share with you as I have with many others over a forty-year career in athletics.

I humbly see myself as a thoughtful, observant teacher and coach with a deep spiritual connection helping me to master my craft. I'm not a Zen Buddhist, but I practice each day how to be a better version of myself by attending to the teachings of the Buddha. I am the hole in a flute through which comes the breath of other brilliant minds, from me to you.

I've been at it for most of my life, and after forty years of coaching, teaching, writing, and performing, I am only halfway there. I am a spiritual seeker, a spiritual wanderer and wonderer seeking out and discovering what appears to make sense of the journey, especially in the world of sports, to which I've been attached at the hip since I discovered a ball at the age of five. I'm trying to figure it out. Sports has been an awesome venue to ask the bigger, deeper questions. Everything I am today has been heavily influenced by sport and my years as a competitive athlete, coach, and teacher.

The Why Factor

To me, *why* I write a book is crucial. There are four reasons why I am writing this book. First, to help you and me to master our crafts. Second, to help us be relevant and important to our family, friends, and teams. Third, to enable us to be valuable contributors to society and make a difference in the lives of others. Fourth, I am writing it not only to create a book, but to feel a sense of fulfillment and satisfaction and bring personal purpose to my life as well as the lives of others. This sustains me, and rather than retire, it helps me to refire and rewire for the creation of a more meaningful life. The following words in accord with Buddhist thought inspire and empower me to stay on task: "Your purpose in life is to find your purpose and give your whole heart and soul to it."

I've given my soul to this book and a big piece of my heart as well. In Simon Sinek's brilliant book *Start with Why: How Great Leaders Inspire Everyone to Take Action*, he states, "People don't buy what you do, they buy why you do it." It's your connection with my why…discovering a sense of self, finding a deep sense of purpose, growing spiritually…that drives you toward what I have written. It is all about making a difference with strong intentions and purpose, and that speaks to why you are reading this book. You enjoy the path that leads to wisdom. That's your *why* as well.

As you remain open and receptive to the wisdom of the Buddha, be sure to do what feels right, following your intuition. It will lead you to much wisdom as you become a more masterful athlete and person in all of your life. One could surely argue that the Buddhist tradition represents the richest source of contemplative wisdom that any civilization has produced—so says Sam Harris, American author, neuroscientist and philosopher.

Along the lines of Harris' assertion, I ask that you consider this advice from Buddhist thought:

"Know well what leads you forward and what holds you back, and walk the path that leads to wisdom."

Part One

WHEN BUDDHA AND SPORTS CONVERGE

Competitive Astronauts of Inner Space

While I did coin the term Buddha Sports, you need to know that the convergence of Buddhism with sports has been a worldwide phenomenon for well over four centuries. Athletes and coaches from Tibet, Japan, Canada, Italy, the United States, and other countries were aware of this sacred union long before I discovered the use of these traditions to create extraordinary performance with my teams and clients for thirty years with great success.

The purpose of this part of the book is to help you to enjoy some entertaining and inspiring examples of those who have chosen the Competitive Buddha way to elicit personal best performances on the journey to becoming the best version of themselves. After all, I open this section with an astute observation from no less of an American sports icon than Michael Jordan, who openly proclaims how this Buddhist stuff really works.

After you read these tales from around the world, maybe you'll become convinced that it really works for you as well.

Here are several of the global competitive astronauts of inner space.

That Zen Buddhist Stuff
Really Works

In one unforgettable instant during the Finals of the 1998
NBA playoffs, Michael Jordan, calm, relaxed, and focused
in the moment, hit "the shot" with seconds left on the game
clock to win the World Championship for the Chicago Bulls.
Recounting that moment, George Mumford, author of the
brilliant book, *The Mindful Athlete*, remembered Jordan's
words: "That Zen Buddhist stuff really works." Mumford,
the master of mindfulness training for the Bulls, had used
Buddhist teachings in a sports context to help the athletes
unlock the competitive game. Michael received what was
perhaps the most endearing, charming compliment from his
arch rival Kobe Bryant, who chided Michael as "Buddha at the
top of the mountain." Kobe embraced the Buddha through
consistent daily meditation practice, a fact of which many of
us who were coached by Phil "Zen Master" Jackson along with
Mumford were aware. So have thousands of other athletes from
throughout the world who have experienced the competitive
Buddha Way for mastery in the arena of sport.

For example, here are a few of the superhuman athletes
who have gravitated to the teachings of the Buddha to achieve
mastery and competitive acumen in their sport. It is first
necessary to understand that Buddhism is all about the mind
and the thoughts and perceptions it manufactures. It is the
mind that separates good athletes from great athletes. Mental
and spiritual skills and talents are what make the difference for
all of us, regardless of one's individual physical talent. These
athletes combine their sports with Buddhist mindfulness
meditation to help create inner calm and peace, leading to the

ability to focus on extraordinary competitive performance. These athletes I refer to as true athletic Buddhas.

Lebron James uses meditation to prepare himself and has been known to quiet his mind during time-outs with "Buddha breathing."

Then there is Derek Jeter, one of the greatest shortstops ever to play baseball. During his seasons as a New York Yankee, he would meditate for an hour at a time.

The LA Dodgers' right fielder Shawn Green, another iconically athletic baseball player, studied Zen Buddhism; according to him, it made him a better person and a better athlete. His Buddhist approach to playing basketball helped him to achieve arguably the greatest single-game statistics in Major League Baseball history. The LA Dodgers were facing the Milwaukee Brewers in the finale of a three-game series. Green went six-for-six that day with six runs, seven RBIs, and a record nineteen total bases.

Olympians Misty May Treanor and Kerri Walsh, two of the best volleyball athletes on a team of all time, practiced yoga and considered meditation as their secret weapon.

The all-time leading scorer in Major League Soccer, Chris Wondolowski of the San Jose Earthquakes, is aligned with the way of the Buddha. Since I've worked closely with Chris, we have had many conversations about a Buddhist approach to his game and how specifically to implement such wisdom on the pitch during practice and in games as a team captain. The work on this we did together had a transformational effect on his experience as an athlete, a captain, and a human being actualizing what he hoped to become.

The late, great, iconic NBA baller Kobe Bryant learned from Phil Jackson and George Mumford how to use meditation prior to a game. Kobe has said, "George helped me to understand the art of mindfulness, to be neither distracted nor focused, rigid nor flexible, passive nor aggressive…I learned to just be."

I learned that Kobe continued to meditate in his retirement each morning. I understood that he read my book *The Way of the Champion* and made it known that he used it and that it really helped him. This book is solidly based on Eastern thought, gathered from both Chinese and Buddhist wisdom.

When the Seattle Seahawks won the 2014 Super Bowl, coach Pete Carroll credited the practice of meditation with having helped them on that remarkable journey.

And I want to mention from my own experience with athletics over the past thirty years that this Buddhist stuff really does work. As a coach, mentor, and teacher, I have guided over a hundred teams to world, national, state, and conference championships in a multitude of sports at all levels of play. I've successfully employed this refreshing approach to help others to develop confidence, mental tenacity, spiritual strength, inspiration, and mastery, both for competitive athletics and in navigating the challenges in all of life.

Magical Monastery Sports

Following in the footsteps of the competitive Buddha is the spiritual sports work of Master Hsing Yun, founder of Fo Guang Shan, the biggest Buddhist monastery ever established, located today in Taiwan. His primary mission when alive was to advance Buddhist beliefs through competitive sports. Master Yun, who lived 1906 to 2005, loved basketball and promoted the Buddha through "hoops." For him, basketball was not just a way of physical training, but a perfect opportunity for practicing mindfulness and the philosophy of the Bodhisattva. Team work, a brave spirit, tolerance, integrity, selflessness, cooperation, and loving your opponents and what they competitively have to offer were some of the philosophical tenets that he taught using the competitive Buddha model.

He also used sports as a way to understand life. Life, he believed, was a ball game; and in this bigger game, you need to follow your heart when competing both on and off the field.

According to Master Hsing Yun, the proper goal of athletics is to apply the wisdom and insight from Zen stories to the challenges of sports. He referred to this process as the practice of Humanistic Buddhism, of how to help one another and work together to achieve something greater than any one individual… the true mission of all competitive sports.

In his groundbreaking global work, he gave full support to competitive sportswomen in basketball, gymnastics, and soccer, going so far as to sponsor them on the international stage to carry out the teachings of Buddha.

In 1997, the renowned baseball teams of Taiwan's Major League came to his monastery to gain a mental edge in competitive athletics. Hsing Yun realized that Buddhism and competitive sports were not mutually exclusive. His programs embraced the humanistic notion that the true meaning of competition was to seek together, to help each other to discover each individual's personal mastery.

In 2009, this magical monastery promoted nationwide sports competition while helping others grasp the lessons of the Buddha on the path of mastery. This movement, which was simply called 'The Three Sports Association,' clearly expressed the essence of what I am saying in *The Competitive Buddha*.

Kung Fu Nuns of Nepal

On the outskirts of Kathmandu, Nepali Buddhist nuns swirl blades, flash swords, punch air, and spin and kick in unison as they complete their daily health movements in an age-old traditional Kung Fu form for warriors. They are proud to be the female athletes of the Himalayas. These spiritual warriors are part of the Drukpa Order, a branch of Himalayan Buddhism. These are not your typical Buddhist nuns who accept the ancient notion of women as second-class citizens. Thanks to the progressive beliefs of their spiritual leader, Gyalwang Drukpa, these great spirits are being placed in leadership roles and educated in the athletic art of Kung Fu. Drukpa believed that sports and physical activity were part of their spiritual growth, and that spiritual growth contributes to their physical process. Through spirituality, these nuns improve their ability to walk, bicycle, and run while boosting their fitness physically and spiritually. These warrior nuns are fearless role models for empowering all women throughout the world. They are dedicated to the service of others.

During the massive earthquake in Nepal that took the lives of almost 10,000 people in 2015, these same warriors were first responders, carrying out helicopter rescues and transporting survivors to safety in huge trucks on high mountain roads. When the dust settled, they helped rebuild many of the homes destroyed in the quake. Drukpa points out how their competitive athleticism and Buddhist nature contributed to their amazing strength during the catastrophe, putting compassion into action. Their Buddhist beliefs help to make them strong, fierce, competitive warriors.

Today, over eight hundred nuns ranging in age from eight to eighty are being empowered and inspired through sports as strides are being made toward gender equality. Having women feel important, valued, and respected is imperative in this branch of Buddhist culture. Because of this, there is now a long waiting list for girls who desire to be part of this revolutionary Kung Fu Nun movement.

Marathon Monks of Mount Hiei

In his classic book *The Zen of Running*, Fred Rohe beautifully addresses the athlete's spiritual path to enlightenment and mastery. He observes how there are no possible victories aside from the joy you experience while dancing your run. These words perfectly describe the *Marathon Monks of Mount Hiei*, the title of John Stevens' famous book. These monks are not hoping to run fast or win a race. They simply hope for spiritual growth as they become one with the sacred Buddhist mountain, dancing effortlessly along the path, free of obstruction in concert with the Buddha Sports way. The joy of this movement is felt in the effortless effort experienced while totally focused on the 'running dance.'

These explorers of inner space are called *gyojas*. A gyoja is a Buddhist spiritual athlete who moves along the path, circling the mountain in search of awareness. The Buddha helps them run; running helps them to awaken; thus, the competitive Buddha journey.

Legend has it that these monks run one thousand marathons (26.2 miles each) in one thousand days—in straw sandals, no less—in their quest to reach enlightenment. At the completion of this journey, the monks spend nine days without food, water, or sleep. Those who succeed become revered as human Buddhas or living saints.

So, what does all this mean to you and me? Well, in Japan, sport is often seen as a path toward self-fulfillment. Sport is simple and pure; it has a power to clear the mind and fill the soul that few other activities possess. Back in the day, as a competitive runner, I had many transformational moments where it felt like I was meeting my maker. Buddhist thought helped me get a better grasp on life and its challenges; it also helped me to be a better athlete. The physical activity helped me to break through emotional blockages as my body began to feel light, fluid, flowing, strong, and at one with the earth beneath my feet. I am always in search of that sacred place; I want to find it once more and bathe in its beauty. I think I'll don my running shoes and head to the trail for another spiritual athletic experience.

Temple in Toronto

Zenji Nio may not be your average everyday household name, yet it belongs to a medalist who is considered godlike by other athletes of the Pan American Games. According to most of those highly competitive athletes, without Nio, they wouldn't have won a medal. His Buddhist temple in Toronto was the biggest attraction in the Pan Am Games village. Within this sacred space, he provided spiritual guidance and counseling, helping many athletes to find individual mastery and win multiple medals in sports such as gymnastics, windsurfing, handball, judo, and rugby. The results achieved using the competitive Buddhist way were an eye-opener for anyone who had the honor of having been in his presence.

Nio was one of several sports chaplains invited to provide such guidance. It was an interfaith operation with Nio representing the Buddhist path. He created a temple not knowing if any athletes would come to it, but as it turned out, his spiritual space was in much demand. As I might have guessed from what I've heard from my athletes, coaches, and teams, Buddhism was extremely popular with many Pan Am Games athletes. Meditation and yoga seem to appeal to all regardless of religious preferences.

The biggest success Nio experienced was with the Brazilian women's rugby team. Prior to the games, no one had picked them for a podium finish. They had several starters sidelined with injuries and were the clear underdogs in the bracket. Nio trained them to be super focused, present, calm, and fearless. Like all great teams, these athletes competed with the mindset that the game was bigger than their individual selves. The competitive Buddha way helped them to put aside fear and negativity and enabled them to compete with faith in their coach and teammates and in themselves. They went on to defeat archrival Argentina 29–0 and captured the bronze medal. This was the impetus for many other athletes and teams to experience the Buddhist way of mastery, thereby finding ways to manage stress and discovering equanimity, spiritual peace, and a sense of meaning beyond the game.

Dancing Kaizen Quakes

My most recent experience of introducing my competitive Buddha approach to inspire leadership, spirituality, and mastery in athletics was with a men's professional soccer team. The San Jose Earthquakes finished dead last in the MLS (Major League Soccer) in 2018. Prior to the start of the 2019 season, the Quakes hired me to assist in the building of a strong, connective, champion sports culture as their psychologist and spiritual advisor.

To that end, I sat with the coaching staff and management and introduced the Japanese concept of *kaizen*, an essential element of Japan's spiritual competitive success, one now recognized worldwide as an absolute necessity in sports, business, and life. Kaizen is about small, gradual, incremental improvement in a safe, cooperative, connected, caring environment where everyone does their share while fulfilling their role. I convinced them that change takes time and that with patience and persistence, we all win, we all gain, and we all experience something miraculous. After all, the Japanese rebuilt their entire culture from complete devastation after World War II to become a global leader in most industries. I also reminded them that iconic Hall of Fame coaches like Bill Walsh, Pete Carroll, Steve Kerr, Brad Stevens, and Anson Dorrance are very much aligned with this special concept of kaizen in their competitive cultures.

With this as a foundational, solid action plan, we moved ahead. We helped the athletes to become competitive Buddhas by increasing their sense of being connected and more selfless, letting go of outcomes and focusing on process, empowering and inspiring each other, and being transparent and genuine. With most of the season completed, we were just two points from ranking in fifth place out of twenty-four teams. When the season finished, we had amassed more than three times more victories than in the previous season using competitive Buddha principles and wisdom.

Here is an example of that wisdom I used in one of my messages, which I call JerEmails:

What a very different season and vibe we are having. Last year, we would never have won that game on Saturday. You never gave up—never. You battled to the very end, believing in yourselves, scoring the winning goal in stoppage time. What I truly love about you all is when that goal was scored, the celebration demonstrated not just the goal, but the joy (one of our Buddha values) of those involved in the score. There was sincere love between all of you warriors. Interesting how the emotional response from a goal gives you all permission to express openly that love we really do share. My point is simple: Let's look for ways to express that true love for each other each day at practice and in the locker room. Don't wait for a certifiable reason such as a goal which has public sanction to let each other know and feel that love. We are brothers, we are family…we win, lose, compete, work, practice, fight, battle together!!! It's that love that gave us that win, that's what Buddha athletes do and how they act.

The other elements that keep us together are the Buddha teachings in respect & humility:

1. *Respect…Great teams operate out of respect, respect for the team's diversity, its differences in personalities, opinions, style, approach, and skill sets. Despite the differences, we must function as a unified* family. *Your diversity is your* greatest strength, *boys!* Unite *behind a common goal, our* why, *which is to be connected, be caring, and make*

a difference in each other's lives. Our goal is to change the status quo of the game so that we can be the class act of the MLS, the standard by which we measure excellence in *futbol. This is our* why: *In addition to experiencing success as warrior athletes, by our* union, *we show the world that we* refuse to give others permission to make us feel less than great. Respect *leads to* trust; trust *leads to* loyalty; *and* loyalty *leads to* love…*the single most powerful Buddha competitive advantage. And* love *leads to a lifetime of true friendship that will enable you to fight and even* die *for each other. I* know *this is true. I saw it when I served in the* Navy *as an officer during the* Viet Nam War. *That's what I observed on Saturday.*

2. Humility *doesn't make you think less of yourself…it makes you think of yourself less. Such is the competitive Buddha way. Arrogance and vanity are counterproductive.* Humility = strength, *not weakness. Humble people know who they are. They realize that who they are and what they become is the result of having been given so much by so many others. I would not be who I am or have achieved what I've achieved had it not been for my wife, kids, and other brilliant people,* and *had it not been for all the* Quakes *and what you continue to give to me every day. It is an honor to be invited into your beautiful lives.*

To make sure that my Buddha message with the athletes was reinforced and had carryover with the staff, I sent the following email to all coaches:

I love working with this team. Here is the message I gave them this week; I told them that in every one of the championship teams I've been with at pro and college level, they had to deal with outside influences that serve no one and distract from our mission. I told them how we must

*not give attention to the media who constantly talk about
needing to win, and I told them not to pay attention to the
standings. Both of these are distractors that take our minds
and hearts away from our mission, which is…to play each
half as a new game, doing all the little things brilliantly
rather than big things marginally.*

*Buddhist thought reminds us to be the warrior and let
go of the suffering caused by our attachment and clinging
to outcomes and results. Suffering is optional, and we
can mitigate it by being the competitive Buddha athletes
we are. I suggest that we not show up to win the game,
but show up to win the day. If we focus on winning these
games, we cannot control things, and that makes us tight
and tense. If we focus on "win the day" as a goal, we can
control that, and we get calm and relaxed and excited.
Winning the day is about daunting defense, attacking
often, and never giving up regardless of score. Never let
the opponent defeat our spirits (our identity), compete like
crazy with our hair on fire, and empower and encourage
each other. We control all this, and it is a choice. Winning
the game cannot be controlled. Notice how this is an
acronym that spells DANCE.*

*I call this Buddha way the "DANCE," the
harmonious gathering of warriors who execute what they
can control and let outcomes take care of themselves. The
"DANCE" is about doing all the above—the controllables.
When in the playoffs, the media and others will talk about
"one and done"…you lose, and you're finished. This puts
focus on negative outcomes and makes us tense. I came up
with a different phrase: "DANCE and advance." All this
we can control, and it's a choice.*

Finally, I wrote:

Fear (fear of making mistakes, of not playing) is the #1 cancer of athletic souls...it weakens us, and we die inside. The cure for this cancer is faith...Faith in a higher power, faith in the Buddha, faith in the system, the staff, and all those things that brought us to this place. Fear is soccer death; faith is soccer life. We either feel fear or we feel free. It's our choice. I then asked them to promise to take it all to heart and not give the media or team standings, points, or others permission to distract from our mission...to compete like crazy together doing what we love to do while loving each other as we do it is the path of mastery. It is being Buddha Nature, the way of Buddha Sports.

From that point on, we had secretly become what I call the 'Dancing Kaizen Quakes.'

The Mindful Women of Maryland Lacrosse

Lacrosse is a sport with deep, sacred, spiritual roots. Its legendary beginnings can be traced to Native American cultures, with their connection to the Great Spirit. Lacrosse is so much more than an athletic game; it is very much recognized as a ceremonial event. As a gift from the creator, it is a sport that is meant to teach the athlete the value of community, family, teamwork, and working together for each other and the greater good while releasing tension and stress with positive energy, enriching the lives of the entire community. Symbolically, the stick used to play the game is referred to as "the cross." When a lacrosse player dies, tradition says that the athlete is buried with their stick, because then they can play in heaven. Thunder is the sound of a lacrosse game in progress, or so it was told in legend.

In 1995, head coach Cindy Timchal of the Maryland women's lacrosse team reached out to me after reading my bestselling book *Thinking Body, Dancing Mind* to ask if I would bring my spirituality of sport message to her team. I couldn't refuse, and that became the start of a twenty-five-year relationship that continues to this day. Using Buddhist, Taoist, and Native American traditions coupled with Western psychology, we managed to master our game on the road to winning seven consecutive national championships, a record that has never been broken. And may I add that the coaching staff, including Cindy Timchal and the legendary Gary Gait, made it all possible by implementing the principles of spiritual competition that I taught.

When I started working to help this storied athletic program, my first act was to introduce everyone to the Buddhist Vipassana tradition of mindfulness meditation. In time, the athletes dedicated themselves to becoming astronauts of inner space. You see, mindfulness (which we'll dive into further in Part Three) is simply being consciously aware of the present moment and our thoughts and actions so that you know what you are doing, how you are doing it, and why. Athletics is the perfect venue for the practice of mindfulness for mastery, leadership, and deepened spirituality in sports and life.

From mindful meditation, we went on to explore and absorb other finer points of Buddhism such as compassion, letting go of outcomes, happiness, being present, selfless teamwork, joy, right speech, preparation, cooperation, right action, and other concepts on the Noble Eightfold Buddhist path. We learned to tame the "monkey mind" and compete more often in the "zone." We in fact often became the game itself, aware of being one with the ball, the stick, the field, and each other for a purpose bigger than any one of us.

This experience of bringing Buddha wisdom to sport and having the freedom to experiment with that was the beginning of my journey, a journey continuing for many years to come, introducing these sacred, spiritual ways to unlock the competitive gate and inspire mastery in 115 championship teams. The goal was not ever to win these championships; the goal was to create safe, spiritually enlightened, and aware environments where the athletes and coaches could maximize their opportunities to approach living life up to their full competitive capacity. That said, there were many other non-championship teams who were successful in this regard. The mindful women of Maryland happened to have not just the spiritual talent but the necessary physical and mental talent as well as awesome coaching to enable them to go the distance each of those championship years.

The Competitive Buddha

I will say this: After all these years, those women still keep in touch with me and tell me how these Buddha truths have helped them to be successful in all of life. Gary, Cindy, and I still work together with a number of different schools. We use the same timeless indomitable Buddha precepts of creating harmony of body, mind, and spirit for physical enjoyment and personal growth and fulfillment as we help ourselves and others to master both competition and the bigger game of life.

In a related but important note, while Cindy left the Maryland program fifteen years ago, present head coach Cathy Reese, who was a student athlete when I began my work there, has continued their winning ways, as the Terps are perennial contenders for the national championship. I have to believe that some of that Buddhist stuff is still in the air on some level, and it really works.

Pacific Buddhist Dragons

Now that I've covered the impact of the competitive Buddha in the professional and collegiate ranks, let me segue into my work delivering the Buddha Sports message to youngsters in high school. Their results show how these concepts are relevant, important, and valuable with all age levels in athletics.

The first high school that comes to mind is actually called the Pacific Buddhist Academy, a one-of-a-kind learning institution located in Honolulu, Hawaii. While I don't work with this school, the essence of their message is preparing the students for an enriched life through Buddhist values. Students of all beliefs and religious backgrounds are welcome; the staff teaches students to think critically while being creative, and open to cooperative collaboration. Some of the basic Buddhist principles included in the curriculum are compassion, mindfulness, gratitude, and self-awareness, including the unity of body, mind, and spirit, especially how these relate to athletics. Basic Buddhist practices such as selflessness, generosity, moral conduct, patience, perseverance, strong effort, and meditation guide student behavior in athletics as well as in classwork.

It is the mission of Pacific Buddhist Academy Athletics to provide a high quality sports program in a caring, nurturing, safe environment. They seek to support these youngsters in developing physically as well as mentally, emotionally, and spiritually. They state how they value athletics and view sports as an integral aspect of a child's overall development. For them, Buddhism and athletics are a perfect marriage to enhance the growth of their students.

I was so impressed by this unconventional program that I purchased a T-shirt bearing their mascot, a Dragon surrounded by the words Pacific Buddhist Athletics, to wear when working with coaches and athletes in other high schools where I coach and teach others to embrace similar Buddhist wisdom.

A perfect example is my work with the Colorado Academy. This beautiful private high school invited me to bring my message to their athletic program. Athletic director Bill Hall is completely on board with my Buddha Sports work with their athletes and coaches. Two Colorado Academy teams I influenced using competitive Buddha wisdom won state championships in girls lacrosse and soccer. I want to give you a sense of how I do this work by retelling the amazing story of my interaction with head coach Sean Stedeford and his soccer girls. Sean has attended several of my Way of Champions coaching conferences and has studied the Buddha Sports way as my client over a two-year period.

In describing an important game, Sean had this to say:

I have never seen my group play like this. There was a mindful purpose to everything they did. They showed caring and stayed connected. [It showed in] how they passed, how they communicated, [and] how they tackled, and the most impressive thing we saw was how they played for one another. They were committed to being connected and a good teammate for the person to their left, right, and behind! For the first time this season, the girls all felt what it was like to play "Buddha ball" and pull in the same direction, and as the game went on, their confidence began to soar! Our Buddha team culture and family mentality were on full display. In the dying moments of the game, it appeared we were about to give the game away when our goalkeeper made one of the most spectacular saves I've ever seen to keep Grandview [the opposing team] out of the goal. The second overtime ended 1–1, and our girls stormed the field like they had just won the state championship. It meant so much to them, I can't put it into words! They played like warriors. What a moment! We definitely "won the day." We saw a championship caliber team on the field and on the bench. Everyone contributed.

The further underlying beauty of this inspirational story is that I've been able to follow this team into the very next season. The story is picked up prior to the last game before the state championship. Sean wrote the following to me:

I write to you tonight with tremendous excitement! We are headed to the 3A State Championship on Tuesday night. The girls had to battle against tough and resilient teams throughout the playoffs and have earned the opportunity to play for a championship. I am so proud of them!

What advice would you give me at this moment to help us focus our attention on competing like the Buddha warriors we are?

In my reply to him, I reassured Sean that the Buddha work we've done is complete and to trust the spirit of these athletes. I suggested he tell them this in his pre-game talk:

"I'm not interested in the outcome… I'm interested in your eagerness to complete like Buddha warriors. Be brave, be tough, be the hardest working team on the pitch and never give up! Have fun and joy as you implement our Buddha plan."

Two days later, I woke up to this joyous email from Sean after his team had won the Colorado 3A Championship in girls' soccer:

What a night! Everything we hold close to our hearts in our program was on display last night. I have never been more proud to be the head coach of this program than I was last night. From the outpouring of motivational texts from the alumni and well-wishes from other coaches in the state to watching the girls "compete with their hair on fire" as you say, [it was] was just incredible. Words cannot describe the pride I feel today. I wanted to help create a moment of everlasting value in the lives of these girls, and I believe that as they begin to reflect on this season, they will see we created more than simply "one" moment. It was a season to remember. I am sad to see it end, but this group will forever have a place in my heart! And I want you to know that we all talked about having compassion for our opponents following our victory. I asked them to imagine how the opponent feels right now and how in life there are many joys and sorrows and that could have been us. This Noble Truth was a huge takeaway from the work we did together, Jerry.

My quick reply was:

Hey Sean, congratulations! You and your team took the Buddha Sports message to heart and followed the Buddha way, knowing that there is no path to a championship... being a champion is the path. Thanks for the opportunity to work with you and influence your spiritual growth and development.

Sean's team at Colorado Academy is one of many others at the high school level of athletics that I've helped using Buddhist wisdom to discover mastery on a daily basis. I want to encourage, inspire, and empower you to use the lessons and stories within this book to help your youngsters discover their Buddha athlete path as well.

Divine Ponytail on the Pitch

What a beautiful, majestic nickname for a majestic Buddha
competitor. Roberto Baggio was a Hall of Fame attacking
midfielder and one of the most iconic soccer athletes of all time.
Dubbed the Divine Ponytail for his Buddhist beliefs as well as
his unusual hair style, Baggio was the only Italian footballer
to score a goal in three World Cups. His accolades include a
laundry list of achievements on the pitch: a global superstar
who was voted fourth in the FIFA's Player of the Century
award, FIFA Player of the Year, and chosen FIFA World Cup
Dream Team. Strangely enough, what many remember about
his storied career is his missed shot in a shootout penalty during
the final game of the 1994 World Cup against Brazil. He took
Italy's last PK and put the decisive kick over the crossbar, giving
Brazil the coveted World Cup title in one of the most amazing
upset moments in World Cup history.

Yet amid his career of victory and defeat, what stood
out most to me was his dedication to his Buddhist beliefs,
the source of the word "Divine" in his famous moniker. As a
result of his human rights activism, this true Buddha athlete
was awarded the 2010 Man of Peace title in recognition of his
charitable work and contributions to social justice and peace.

The story of Roberto Baggio is not the tale of a failed
penalty kick. Without Baggio, Italy would never have been in
that final. The real story is how his Buddhist wisdom helped
him to handle his major setback with serenity and equanimity.
His Buddhist training enabled him to maintain his composure
when all seemed hopeless.

He was introduced to the wisdom of Buddhism following
a severe injury in 1987. He became a practicing Buddhist on
a team of Catholics. He continues to use meditation as a way

to become aware of life's meaning and develop the strength to face challenges as they arise. As an act of complete dedication to his Buddhist beliefs in 2014 in Milan, Baggio inaugurated the opening of the largest Buddhist temple in Europe to help others to discover what he has found.

In an article in the Irish Times in 1999, Baggio was given yet another name: the Buddha of Milan. In the piece, Baggio describes the relationship between Buddhism and soccer: "I believe that the most important thing is to be well, inside yourself in your soul. If you are at peace with yourself, you can do anything well. Buddhism has helped me find this inner happiness. With Buddhism, my game has improved—everybody has noticed, coaches, teammates, and fans." The convergence of Buddha with sport enabled him to unlock the competitive gate for his athletics and his life.

Buddha and the Bulls

When you saw the title of this section, you undoubtedly knew who this was going to be about. So did Rev. Noriaki Ito, head of the Higashi Honganji Buddhist Temple in the Little Tokyo section of Los Angeles, an avid "hoop-head" from the time he was a little boy.

Indeed, I am referring to the "Zen Master," one of head coach Phil Jackson's affectionate nicknames, one given to him by sports writers. What sets Phil apart from most sports coaches is his use of mindfulness and Buddhist wisdom, making him one of the most innovative coaches in athletics. His competitive Buddhist ways have become his legendary trademark style. According to Ito, coach Jackson is "a true martial arts master who realizes that the spiritual, mental, and physical have to be integrated into one. I notice more of a focus on denying individual egos for the benefit of the team. In Buddhism, suppressing the ego is central to any kind of awakening." Ito also credits Jackson with helping his athletes explore their inner space in order to know themselves better, to learn their strengths and weaknesses and how important the process of the game is as well as the outcome. Like all of my Buddha athletes, the ultimate mission isn't so much winning but how well the team competes, connects, cares, and loves one another. Such self-awareness is a crucial aspect of Buddhist thought for mastery of leadership and integrating spirituality into sports and life.

From both my working relationship and my friendship with Phil, I can say that his spiritual beliefs merge two disciplines. I would say with some confidence that he considers himself to be a Zen Christian, leaning on each school of thought where appropriate. His Christian background is linked to being the son of fundamentalist Christian preachers; he believes in prayer and miracles.

I also know that he has long been fond of the teachings of the Buddha and the Chinese Way of the Tao. While coaching, Phil had a habit of handing out books to his athletes to help them address their personal and performance issues. I was honored when he would give copies of my books to players like Michael Jordan, Steve Kerr, Kobe Bryant, and others to impart a broad spiritual perspective on the game and life to them.

But as I recall, it was Shunryu Suzuki's *Zen Mind, Beginner's Mind* that was Phil's initial guide to the practice of Zen Buddhism. From there, he was able to apply his learning from his heart to the court. Both of his books, *Sacred Hoops* and *Eleven Rings*, demonstrate his growth as a teacher of Buddhist wisdom as applied to the game of basketball. For example, the patented triangle offense is very Buddha-like, with its continual fluid, flowing, free patterns of movement. From the lens of the Buddhist virtue of selflessness, we can observe how with every championship he won as head coach, he managed to galvanize a team of athletes, who often tend to be self-absorbed, to create unity. Loss and gain, for Jackson, were nothing more than life's cycle of events. He chose what the Buddha called the Middle Path, a more balanced approach to better cope with the suffering of unpredictable outcomes. As a result, he could enjoy the sounds of many hands clapping in victory or learn from the sounds of silence of one hand clapping that accompany a defeat. And finally, compassion, a foundational cornerstone of Buddhist wisdom, is a virtue that Phil believed enabled the Buddha Bulls to sustain high levels of competitive mastery along with compassion for each team member, including self-compassion.

Phil Jackson has won more championships than any coach in professional sports by believing in his unconventional Buddha way. Such a compassionate approach helped his players to trust, connect, and care for each other, enabling them to devote themselves to something perhaps greater than even the game of basketball itself. This is the competitive Buddha way that awakens mastery, leadership, and spirituality within all of us.

The Way of the Tiger

Tiger Woods was born into and raised in the Buddhist tradition, and has publicly stated that his understanding of the Buddha has been the secret to his golfing success. From a very young age, his ability to focus was instilled by his Thai Buddhist mom, Kultida Woods. Supposedly, Tiger slept near a statue of Buddha growing up and even wore a Buddha necklace.

The Buddha Tiger was able to manage all performance anxiety and fear and establish a positive sense of self and peace almost as if he was a Buddhist monk walking the fairways. It has been said that every facet of his athletic dominance could be traced to his solid Buddhist education. From tee box to hole, his mental and spiritual talents are palpably apparent as he demonstrates the "relaxed intensity" of the Buddha himself.

Meditation (see Part Three), a way to develop awareness, kindness, focus, and wisdom, has always been an important part of his game and life, particularly during those challenging times when his life unraveled due his serial infidelity, leading to his divorce. Buddhism helped him to pick up the pieces amid all the pain, and he made a public apology admitting that he had lost his deep connection to his Buddhist way. Yet this up and down path is all part of the Buddha way, which always includes new beginnings after setbacks, whether it be a missed putt, a missed career opportunity, or a missed relationship. The lesson for Tiger was to repent and ask for forgiveness and then start again. And so he did, as he brilliantly does after every flub on the fairway.

In his penetrating, profound book *Tiger Virtues*, Alex Tresniowski writes about Tiger's strong connection to Buddhist wisdom and how relevant it has been with every single shot. In the book, Tresniowski details deep spiritual principles relating

The Competitive Buddha

to being present, being prepared, and the impermanence of success, as well as tenacity, effort, patience, fearlessness, humility, intuition, balance, vision, adaptability, and inner stillness and how all of these virtues impacted the athleticism of Tiger Woods...the Way of the Tiger.

Yet the most impactful virtue was the virtue of positive thinking. Buddhist thought suggests that our lives are shaped by our minds: We are what we think. Tiger examined his own shortcomings and changed the narrative, making it a more proactive, positive, forward-moving story. At one point in this book, the author generously quotes me from my bestseller *Thinking Body, Dancing Mind*: "The words you choose to cultivate in yourself as an athlete will determine your identity and beliefs about yourself...so hopefully those words are positive." Tiger's positive thinking manifests itself both during rounds of golf and afterwards.

The competitive way of this Tiger is through a positive mind, a beginner's mind, the nonjudgmental mind of a Buddha. But know this—while Tiger was not always able to think positively, he was able to do it a higher percentage of the time than most of us. He simply refuses to beat himself up. When asked by a reporter what qualities he didn't like about himself, he responded that he didn't know: "I am constantly evolving." Tiger is the quintessential Buddha athlete.

Part Two

BUDDHA BRAIN, MAMBA MIND

Timeless Values to Inspire Mastery

I was smack dab in the middle of writing this section when I received the heartbreaking news that Kobe Bryant left this world, along with his daughter, Gianna, and seven other friends, in a devastating helicopter crash. This unfortunate loss awakened a sense in me of how Kobe was himself more of a Buddha than most ever knew. I immediately had the thought that I wanted somehow to honor his life as well as his mission, which was to have a positive impact on the world of the female athlete. I chose to take various aspects of his character and mentality and integrate them into the content of this book in an appropriate way. I was talking to one of Kobe Bryant's close friends recently, George Mumford, and he encouraged me to follow through with this idea, to just come from my heart and let my intuition do the writing with no pretension, putting my ego aside. The outcome was the new title for this pivotal section, Part Two. By doing this, I hope to promote Kobe Bryant's legacy and inspire you to embrace what is now called the "Mamba Mentality," a variation on the theme of *The Competitive Buddha.*

Let me begin this section with a word about the Buddha Brain, which believes that life and performance in sports is all about our thoughts. If you change your thoughts, you change your life and performance. If you wish to take charge and experience mastery, your thoughts must align with your vision. In this section, I present impeccable, time-honored Buddhist truths that will influence your thoughts and help create an environment of mastery that supports that vision. But something else is essential to achieve mastery. You must connect the Buddha Brain with the power of the Mamba Mind.

Where the brain is the physical organ in the head that manufactures all thought, the mind is the physical brain plus the body, the world you inhabit, and all of your essential being and culture coming together to produce your mentality, a mindset that helps define masterful performance. It is a behavioral package that results in particular ways of going about a certain task. This is where the Mamba Mind gets interesting.

As a concept, the Mamba Mentality had early roots in Kobe's long-ago tour to Asia where he was observed hanging out with monks at a Buddhist temple. This experience inspired him to lay the foundations of his personal practice of mindfulness and other teachings of Buddhist thought, which would carry over to the day he died. In Kobe's words, "The

Mamba Mentality is not about seeking results, it's about the process of getting to the result... It's all about the journey." Kobe proclaimed that the Mamba Mind is a "constant quest to be the best version of yourself," which is in full alignment with what *The Competitive Buddha* is all about. Kobe has said that the Mamba Mentality is "the ultimate mantra for the competitive spirit."

During Kobe's long career, his brain was apparently marinated in most of the Buddhist values that I present in this section, thanks to his connection with Phil Jackson and George Mumford. Kobe therefore developed a way of performing on the court and in life, and he brilliantly labeled it the Mamba Mentality. This mentality drove him on a constant quest to find answers; he had an endless curiosity to figure things out. His approach, like Buddha Sports athletes, was all about the process and his belief and trust in the wisdom of diligence; he worked hard. He refused to harbor fear about results and focused instead on the Buddhist concept of being present right now. He believed in intentional practice. It didn't matter what others thought about him. He followed the teachings of the Eightfold Path, especially Right Action, Right Thought, Right Effort, Right Livelihood, Right Mindfulness, and Right View. In order to perfect his craft, he acted with faith of his convictions. Kobe was an unusual person who took refuge his entire adult life in his practice of daily meditation. His intention was to practice being the best version of himself daily, one of the strongest hallmarks of the Buddha athlete.

The Mamba Mind is the Zen mind or beginner's mind, and it is made up of the values and thoughts found in this section. It is a child's mind, free of judgment, free of fear, and free of expectation. When athletes and others experience this mindset, they feel a sense of divine liberation. It is only when we control our Buddha Brain thoughts that the state of mastery can be attained.

The Path of Mastery

Speaking of mastery, here are a few thoughts to better help you to gain a perspective on the Buddha Sports concept of mastery. There is no path to mastery; mastery is the path. It is a state of mind achieved through a consistent day-by-day lifestyle of high-level, intentional practice of your sport or other activity. In Buddhist teaching, practice is the way of mastery. The path is often a thousand miles or more, but it begins with a single, high quality first step of intentional preparation. Focusing on this single act alone is considered a step toward mastery. And that movement is repeated over and over and over until you feel it is time to move ahead.

Practice as if you are preparing for the national championship or perhaps for an important talk or presentation. Prepare as if it were your last chance to prove your level of competency. It takes courage to prepare consistently in practice with game time levels of mastery and intensity. The Buddha Brain and Mamba Mind will help you to achieve this.

Mastery means "time in the saddle," preparation that is consistent, gradual, continual, and intentional. It is a principle easily learned. I prepared well to write this book by diligently exercising my Buddha Brain and Mamba Mind for thousands of hours over a thirty-year span. However, this can only be accomplished when there is love, passion, and joy for the work you do. Kobe had this in his life. Mastery in all of life is only possible when these three heartfelt values are present. When they are, the sky's the only limit and you experience mastery.

Happiness: Ephemeral Fix

"Happiness starts with you; not with your relationships,
not with your job, not with your money, but with you."
—Buddhist Thought

From a Buddhist perspective, the pursuit of happiness as a
goal in itself is foolish because of its transient nature, which is
dependent on several uncontrollable conditions. We cannot
transcend the vicissitudes of nature. To live life—to play
sport—is to experience all the joy and bliss along with the
sorrow and disappointment, ephemeral states brought on by
thoughts and perceptions of the Buddha Brain. I've been part
of 115 championship teams, and the bliss typically lasts for only
three days or so. And I've been on the other end of the spectrum
of devastating loss, and within forty-eight hours, things were
back to normal. The sight of freshly fallen snow on a landscape
is gorgeous—only to turn to wet dirty slush in two days.

So it is with happiness. Buddhist thought suggests that
happiness is a *state of mind*, like so much in life. It is an
ephemeral experience that comes and goes. The "happy fix"
never lasts. A new car gets dirty, dusty, and dented. A bike gets
stolen. Shirts wear out and shoes get holes. My take on these
thoughts is that our cravings, desires, wishes, and dreams are the
cause of stress, disappointment and suffering. The key to enter a
more consistent happy space is to place our focus on giving and
serving. Selflessness takes practice.

The Dalai Lama reminds us to not just be selfless, but to
be compassionate toward others and toward yourself. Working
with coaches and athletes, I discuss with them the need for
compassion in their lives if they hope to experience happiness
in sport. (See the next subsection for more on compassion.)

Athletes suffer a great deal, whether over a defeat or loss or the suffering felt as the result of deep fear about whether or not they will win.

On happiness, I tell others that if they want to optimize their chances of feeling happy, be in the moment, think not about the past or future, and let go of the following:

- Always having to be right
- Trying to control everything
- Blaming and pointing fingers
- Criticism
- Negative self-talk
- Limiting beliefs
- Whining and complaining
- Resistance to change
- Labeling others
- Expectations
- Irrational fears

Letting go of any or all of these will not only raise your level of happiness but your level of performance. While you can be happy and not perform well, if you want to perform well, you must be happy. And in the words of the Buddha, there is no path to happiness; happiness is the path. As is true with the Mamba Mind, process is the key to opening the door of happiness.

Compassion: Cultivating an Open Heart

"We need compassion and human affection; they are the ultimate sources of success in life."

—The Dalai Lama

Compassion is a major theme throughout Buddhist teaching; it brings us inner strength, lessens fear, and increases self-confidence, leading to our success in sports and life. It is something that can be taught and therefore learned through consistent and conscious intentional practice.

According to Buddhist thought, compassion is a state of mind of wanting others to feel free, happy, confident, and successful. Isn't this what we all crave for each other in athletics? Coach Phil Jackson agrees and believes that compassion had been the most integral, important aspect of his coaching. He found that a few kind, thoughtful words can have a strongly positive transformative effect on an entire team. He considered it one of several elements responsible for his championship cultures. When Michael Jordan and Kobe Bryant became compassionate leaders, they transformed the Bulls and Lakers into two of the greatest teams of all time. For Phil, Michael, and Kobe, compassion was the key foundational building block in their competitive sports world. Compassion is an essential characteristic of the Mamba Mentality.

It's no accident that coach Steve Kerr of the Golden State Warriors has thoughts about compassion in sports, since Phil was his mentor while playing with the Bulls. One of Steve's core values for the Warriors is *compassion*; he believes that the most powerful leaders in the world are the ones who have enormous compassion for others. Coach Kerr also experienced compassion with head coach Gregg Popovich as a player with the San Antonio Spurs. I've talked with Steve about *compassion* as a cultural value. He believes, as does Jackson, that players respond wholeheartedly to a more compassionate environment both in their reactions, such as when they get to play or don't, and in their understanding of their roles, as well as of each other. As a great communicator, Kerr actively demonstrates his understanding of his players' concerns, issues, and what matters most to them. As a result of this approach, all the Warriors feel that they are valued, important, and relevant regardless of their particular talents.

Pete Carroll, head coach of the Seattle Seahawks, demonstrates an intuitive sense of *compassion* in his championship culture. *Compassion* is not a concept that's often discussed in the NFL, but it is one of the characteristics that Seahawk players most admire about Coach Carroll. It enabled them to connect deeply, and genuine connection is a vital element in cultures that lead athletes to success.

Buddhism's teaching of *compassion* is extremely compelling and applicable to athletics. Buddhist culture is intent on cultivating an open, unlimited heart toward humanity. The Chinese ancient book, the *Tao Te Ching*, states, "Leaders whose positions are lasting are those who are most compassionate; when two armies meet, the one with *compassion* is the one who tastes the 'victory.'"

Such thought is extremely relevant in the current world of sports. Where there is *compassion*, there is courage within, giving a person a sense of comfort and security and the knowledge that if risks are taken, all will be fine regardless of outcome. For example, *compassion* helps you to not worry about mistakes, failures, or loss. *Compassion* helps athletes to learn from setbacks and move on. *Compassion* also empowers you to be brave, fearless, and tenacious.

Missy Foote, winner of four national championship games as head women's lacrosse coach at Middlebury College, shared her wisdom about the value of compassion in a champion culture with me in these words:

> *The most important quality we can share within a team (or a community or family) is to value one another's differences as much as we value our similarities. We each bring our unique selves as we work together toward a common goal of being our best selves, both individually and collectively. Seeing the best in each other and talking about it publicly helps others (and ourselves) recognize our potential. What we need is to recognize our commonalities—that we are all human, and we all have hopes and dreams—emphasizing our similarities despite differences, whether it's a style of play, a way of thinking, or a lifestyle.*

I would like to say a few words about self-compassion in sports. Far too many individuals forget the value of this concept, and in my work with teams, I try to make sure we all understand what it's about. Are you constantly judging yourself, comparing yourself to others, holding yourself to unreasonable standards or to other people's expectations? Are you beating yourself up, putting yourself down, or limiting your peace and happiness by limiting your self-love? We must practice self-compassion. *Compassion*—both for self and for others—is an immensely powerful and peace-loving tool. This state of mind alters brain frequencies, which affects neurophysiology and thus causes physical states to be more relaxed, yet robust and energetic. Know this: We are all human, we make mistakes, and we learn from them. If we're not in the place that we want to be, but we know that we could be, that's okay! What's the rush? We have long lives to live and love and accomplish; we are just where we're supposed to be right now.

So hold yourself a bit more lightly. Your life is indeed an important and meaningful matter, but that doesn't mean you must take it so seriously all the time. Smile to yourself, right now. Laugh, in fact, at the silliness of being so serious. We're here to have fun and to love—both ourselves and others. To love requires patient understanding as well as easy, unconditional caring—indeed, true compassion. You deserve patience and care; you are worthy of being loved. Remember, there's only one *you* in this world. Cherish and honor that unique being.

The Competitive Buddha

Egolessness:
Disguise the Diamond

"When we give up our images of self-importance
and our ideas of what should be, we can help
things to become what they need to be."

—Benjamin Hoff

In his classic work *Zen in the Art of Archery*, Eugene Herrigel comments on how a student swordsman may approach the level of mastery or greatness: "The more he tries to make the brilliance of his swordplay dependent on his own reflection… the more he inhibits the free working of the heart… How does sovereign control of technique turn into master swordplay? Only by the pupil's becoming purposeless and egoless. He must be taught to be detached not only from his opponent but from himself."

Some incredibly talented athletes possess all the skills to make it big, yet they fall short. Often, their ego involvement becomes an obstacle, causing friction between them and other athletes. Much energy is wasted in defending their "greatness," both physically and emotionally. They don't support, cooperate, or encourage their athletic colleagues, and they get none in return because they alienate their teammates with the harshness of their egocentric posture.

The competitive Buddha way to inner power and recognition is to detach from the need for such power. The less you focus upon your greatness in relation to others, on how well you play compared with your teammates or competitors, the more effective and appreciated you will become.

Egocentricity is a hindrance to performance. The constant need to live up to self-centered illusions creates unnecessary and inhibiting anxiety and tension. The athlete who needs to boast and impress others is usually doing so out of feelings of deep insecurity and uncertainty and is wasting a lot of energy.

Egoless Buddha athletes understand that the less they focus on themselves, the more effective they are. Championship teams conceal their advantages and downplay their previous excellent performances, thereby diminishing the chance of counterforce emerging. They appear reserved and humble. They are quiet. Giving the appearance of being almost weak, or at least nonthreatening, has helped many teams overcome apparently stronger teams that actually squander their energies in displays of false dominance.

Your real power as a Buddha athlete comes when you relate to others from your heart rather than your head. The following thoughts will help you to focus your approach toward others with less egocentricity:

- When you are with your team, other athletes, or really anyone, rather than focusing on the impression you're creating on them, concentrate on trying to discover the greatness within *them*. What traits do they possess that you admire?

- Ask yourself how you can be kinder and more considerate. This is true strength and power, since "Soft is strong."

- Look for opportunities when you can sincerely affirm others during practice, after games, and in the locker room. Tell them how much you appreciate and respect them. Ask them questions about things important to them. Make them feel valued, important, and relevant.

- Before you talk about your accomplishments, advantages, or achievements to others, ask yourself what good it will do for others to hear of these. A legitimate, non-ego-related purpose would be to help them to see that they too can achieve—that they are as good as you. If others ask you about yourself, remember that there is only a fine line between reporting and boasting.

According to the Buddha Brain, when the ego dies, the soul awakens and things can become what they need to be. Soul awakening is the essence of the Buddha athlete.

Detachment: Elusive Butterfly

"You can only lose what you cling to."

—Buddhist Thought

A young boy received a butterfly net for his birthday. On a hot, humid summer day, he ran wild trying to catch one of those elusive aviators. After much tension and anxiety from many futile attempts, he fell to the ground in exhaustion. While quietly resting in the grass, he detached from his frustrating quest; and then a butterfly landed on his nose.

I think about this story every time I suffer from wanting what I don't have or having what I don't want. The Buddha knows that the source of our problems is found in attachment. Detachment is the path of peace and happiness. Pay attention, be aware, and don't cling.

It doesn't mean you must give up your goals. You just need to keep your intentions pure, positioning yourself to achieve them, but giving up your attachment to the outcome—releasing your deep need and desire. When you calm down, relax and let go, it ironically becomes easier to get the outcome we originally wanted. This is illustrated by the story about the butterfly above: The boy stayed in the field, let go of the need to capture the insect, and won his heart's desire.

The psychology and physiology of it all is simple. When you let go of the need to win, score points, and improve your stats, the body becomes less tense, less tight, less tentative, and less stressed.

The resulting condition of being relaxed and calm facilitates higher levels of competitive sports performance.

Detachment quiets the ego and opens the heart to extraordinary levels of energy, awareness, joy, and power. Let

The Competitive Buddha

go of your attachment to winning and achievement, and they will come your way. Athletes often report that when they let go during an event, they felt injected with reserves they didn't know they had as a result. To this point, I recall the words of Buddhist teacher Thich Nhat Hanh:

> "Letting go gives us freedom, and freedom is the only condition for happiness. If in our heart we still cling to anything, we cannot be free."

By limiting desire for possessions, praise, and other external attachments, one creates enormous personal power. Athletes who are overly attached to winning medals and trophies, prize money, sponsorships, and accolades are at a great disadvantage, because such ephemeral desires create much tension and pressure, which interfere with the joy, fun, and fulfillment of performance. Detaching from these external desires reduces tension and improves performance.

Detachment doesn't mean that you cease to care about a sporting event. You still care immensely about how you play when you detach from ego concerns—the process itself is characteristic of the Mamba Mentality, and it is important as a vehicle for growth and discovery of what you can and can't do. The outcome is a gauge that measures your level of improvement—accept it for what it truly is. Detachment means letting go of all the ego inflation that we attribute to success. A loss—or a victory, for that matter—is never a measure of your self-worth as an athlete or a person. By practicing detachment, your perspective on your sport is healthier. You can love it with passion, yet see it as only a microcosmic event in a universe of activity. Whether an outcome seems positive or negative, your emotional attachment to it is a setup for disappointment and pain. Consider this classic story:

A very old Chinese man and his young son lived during a period of much civil strife. They were considered rich by the villagers because they owned a horse. One morning, the son awoke to find his horse had run away. Running to his father, the son informed him of this tragedy, saying that this was the worst thing that could have happened. His father in all his wisdom replied, "Is that so? How do you know what it means?" The next day, as the boy was working in the barn, he heard the sound of horses galloping in the distance. When he looked up, he saw his horse leading a herd of wild ponies toward him. Seeing this, he ran to the house shouting, "The horse has come back leading a herd. This is the greatest thing that's ever happened!" In all his wisdom, the old man replied once again: "Is that so? How do you know what it means?" That afternoon, the boy decided to tame one of the ponies. As he proudly sat atop the newfound gift, the horse bucked, throwing the boy to the ground, leaving him with a broken collarbone and a fractured arm. As he was placed in his bed by his father, the boy said, "All those horses coming—that's the worst thing that could have happened." Once again, the old man spoke: "Is that so? How do you know what it means?" The next day, father and son were abruptly awakened by the sound of militia knocking on their door. They were here to take the boy away to fight in the civil war that was happening. The old man said, "There he is, take him." The captain took one look and said, "He's useless to us," and left. The boy said, "This is the best luck I've ever had." And the old man in his wisdom replied, "Is that so? How do you know what it means?"

How do any of us know the real meaning of any single outcome in business and in life? Buddhist thought teaches us to stay in the "now," to be with what is happening, and to detach from judging outcomes. Clinging creates tension, anxiety, and fear. When you let go, you experience a freedom, a sense of relief. As an athlete, if you let go of desire, you can experience more joy and success, as well as an increase in personal freedom enabling you to take more risks in sport without feeling paralyzed by fear of risking. Such freedom allows you to dance and compete in a way that is uninhibited, the way it was meant to be.

In what way is the story of the boy and his horse relevant to you, your sport, and your life? Think of a real-life situation that mirrors this story.

Karma: Cycle of Cause and Effect

"Don't take revenge. Let karma do all the work."
—Buddhist Thought

Often misunderstood, karma is a Sanskrit word that translates to action, whether physical or mental. It is a core concept in the Buddhist tradition. It generally refers to the universal cycle of cause and effect: Like causes produce like effects. For example, good acts lead to a future good effect; a bad deed will lead to a future harmful effect. Karmic principles apply to one's work, thoughts, and actions, which are all "deeds." And the intention behind each action matters as well. For example, I may praise someone with the ulterior intention to win their approval. This is a good action for the wrong reason.

And karma can be changed. Essentially, you free yourself from bad karma by living your life in accordance with your own divine guidance, listening within. When you observe the laws of nature (see epilogue) and the Noble Eightfold Path (see Part Three), you begin to act in ways congruent with what is right.

Karma and sports are, like all of life, interconnected. Athletes can begin to learn that taking negative action into the competitive arena will ultimately lead to payback, if not immediately, then later. For example, when you commit a foul in sports. you receive a penalty on the spot if the official witnesses it. You may pull on the opponent's shirt and get away with it for now, leading to a victory because of that action. But then driving home from the event, your conscience prevents you from celebrating and you feel guilty. That is a kind of karma. Cheating in sports is something that eventually catches up to you. And your good deeds of encouraging your teammates and staff often create positive results, causing you to get praise back from others. Putting in the extra work pays off as well.

It has been said that the quality of the seeds you plant and the quality of the soil will determine the quality of the crop harvested. Karma is about reaping the harvest we have planted through our thoughts, words, and actions.

> "My actions are my only true belongings. I cannot escape the consequences of my actions. My actions are the ground upon which I stand."
> —Thich Nhat Hanh

Impermanence:
What Rises Will Fall

"It is not impermanence that makes us suffer. What makes us suffer is wanting things to be permanent when they are not."

—Thich Nhat Hanh

There is only one constant in life and that is that change will happen. The seasons of the year, the cycles of weather, the journey of life and death, the rising of the sun and the setting of the moon all show us that impermanence is a fact of life. Many practitioners understand such the changeable nature of what is as the cornerstone of Buddhist teachings. Nothing lasts, and our futile attempts to hold onto things are the root of much suffering. The wisdom of Buddhist thought suggests, "Impermanence is inescapable; all things vanish. Time itself is impermanent."

In my life, I have experienced sadness and loss; yet in time, these periods gave way to joy and gain, only to return back to sadness and loss once again. Life fluctuates. The Buddha reminds me that life is ten thousand joys, ten thousand sorrows, for all of us. Nothing is endless bliss or joy. There is social injustice and simple struggle with how unfair life seems to be. As searing as the loss of a friend or a defeat in the sports arena may be, my tears in response to such an event arise out of deep love. All loss and challenging changes in life deepen my ability to connect with passion and love.

I remember the joy, excitement, and bliss of being intimately involved in seven consecutive women's lacrosse championships at the University of Maryland. The athletes, coaches, and myself thought we'd never lose. Then it happened; several years of not hoisting the trophy. We were in a state of shock and disbelief, since we had gotten into the habit of thinking our streak would never end. The program has come full circle, and these days the Terps are back on top, winning championships with regularity once again. This, too, will change.

Such swings from dominance to mediocrity or irrelevancy are just the way it is in sports. Who remembers the dominating Boston Celtics of the 1950s to the '60s? Most recently, the Golden State Warriors have gone from being perennial champions to having close to the worst record in the NBA.

Because of his Buddhist childhood, Tiger Woods understands the impermanence of success. After years of being at the top, he now struggles to get a victory; what goes up must come down.

I have been grappling recently with the decline of my running speed. People pass me on the hills where that never used to happen before. I'm experiencing the cycle of age and diminishing physical capability. While it's not easy, I do realize this is the never-ending swing of life and performance. Nothing lasts forever, not high times nor low. The key is to appreciate every day we have, knowing this too will change. The competitive Buddha is well aware of this.

When you take a good look at your world of athletics, there is nothing to cling to. Your grasping to hold on to results and outcomes is continually challenged.

Athletics, like life, is a continually moving pendulum, a never-ending process constantly recycling itself. If you don't like a situation, know that in time, it will change. All you can do at any moment is focus on what you have (rather than what you lack) and how you will make the most of that, doing the best you can to get the most out of your experience. Discover the gem inside the darkness.

By embracing impermanence profoundly, you become free and liberated. This entails letting go, not of your efforts, your work ethic. or your wish to master your craft, but of resistance to the constant change and impermanence of life—letting go of your desperate need to control it all. Buddhist teacher Ajahn Chah reminds us, "If you let go a little, you'll have a little peace. If you let go a lot, you'll have a lot of peace. If you let go completely, you'll have complete peace."

> "In the end these things matter most: How well did you love? How fully did you live? How deeply did you let go?"
> —Buddhist Thought

Selflessness: From Me to We

"If you knew what I know about the power of giving, you would
not let a single meal pass without sharing it in some way."

—Buddhist Thought

Buddhism is the way of selflessness. It is selfishness that leads
to suffering. According to the competitive Buddha, the only
way we can live fully and enjoy life is to know that our purpose
in this life is to serve. A life of self-absorption rarely goes well.
Giving to others gives us a deeper sense of peace, joy, and
happiness. Basically, it feels so good to give. In his later years
as an athlete, Kobe understood the value of giving to others on
his team and in life as well. Selflessness was a significant aspect
of the Mamba Mentality. Witness his total involvement in the
development of female athletes and their sports world.

Selflessness is the one core value that has permeated the
hearts of every one of my championship teams, and that
holds true to this day. In a conversation with iconic basketball
coach Dean Smith, he told me how basketball is a game
about unselfish acts, giving, and serving. He taught me how
selflessness brings out the best in everyone.

It's not easy being selfless in today's world, where so many
athletes are overly concerned with what they are getting—more
playing time, more recognition, more money. My favorite
story to tell about athletes and selflessness is one about Andre
Igoudala of the Golden State Warriors. Evidently, when Steve
Kerr took over as head coach with the Warriors organization,
one of his first acts was to talk with Andre about his role on
the team. Andre, an NBA All-Star and a consistent starter on
every team he played for in every game of his career, was asked
by Kerr how he'd feel if he didn't start with the Warriors and

instead would just come off the bench when needed. Kerr told him how that would make the team even better. Andre unselfishly responded that he would agree to do whatever was best for the team. He trusted Kerr and contributed to his team in this way all season. Subsequently, Andre was called upon to start in the Finals of the 2015 Championship series, and his stellar performances earned him recognition as the MVP of those Finals as the Warriors won their first championship with Steve Kerr. Arguably, all this happened because Andre selflessly chose to be an example of the competitive Buddha athlete.

In accord with the high priority Kerr puts on selflessness, his players find joy in giving to each other. Kerr states that the concept of *selflessness* is counterintuitive in professional sports, where many worry about getting enough—money, playing time, statistics, recognition, etc. Yet Kerr finds a way to create a giving culture. His method is to ask players to be mindful of giving to each other as a way to ultimately get more in return. Notice how unselfishly they distribute the ball, throw an extra pass, and give credit to others for their contribution.

In his bestselling book *Sacred Hoops*, Phil Jackson talks about surrendering the "me" for the "we," a system that inspired and empowered everyone, athletes, staff, and management. It was a system defined by the famous triangle offense, a strategy that demanded they put the needs of the team before their own. This was quite a challenge to execute with professional superstars in the NBA. The Bulls mastered this concept, resulting in a powerful group intelligence greater than any one athlete on the team. And most of the players would agree that their team winning six national championships was intricately tied to their selfless culture.

The Competitive Buddha

I leave you with this thought from the Dalai Lama:

"Our prime purpose in this life is to give to and help others."

When you do, you thrive. We are on this planet to do one thing: Serve. Ask yourself today, how can I bring more to life by serving another person?

Patience: Go Slower,
Arrive Sooner

*"Be patient. Everything comes to you at the right
moment. The greatest prayer is patience."*
—Buddhist Thought

In my selfish, impatient view, the rest of the world needs to
catch up to me. It is also this perception that causes me endless
and unnecessary suffering. Patience is the virtue I fail to master.
And what is worse is that I want to have patience *now* and do
not want to wait any longer. Surely you see the irony in this last
sentence; it speaks to the gravity and urgency of my problem.

Well, I'm happy to tell you my level of self-compassion
is helping me to be more patient each day, accepting most of
those things that can annoy me in the present moment. I am
feeling more peaceful and less anxious. I attribute this shift in
consciousness to my daily meditation practice, which helps me
to be more mindful of this issue and accept what is. It's not like
my impatience is permanently gone, but I do feel good about
how I can catch it early as it begins to appear. I take three deep
breaths and remind myself how I'd rather be happy than right.
Being aware of my impatience has been the key to managing it.

Patience is an important virtue for those of us in athletics.
We want success, and we want it now. We want to play more,
earn more, and get more and more—and we do not want to
wait. This makes us tight, tense, and tentative, which in turn
delays what we desire to have happen.

As suggested in the opening quote, Buddhist thought
teaches that all things come at the appropriate time. Patience
is the ability to enjoy and immerse yourself in the process, the
flow of life, as it assumes its own form and shape. I use the

The Competitive Buddha

following story to demonstrate the importance of patience and mastery in sports:

> *An athlete went to her coach and asked how long it would take to develop into a world-class triathlete. He reassured her that if she trained properly, it would take four to five years to come into her own. Feeling frustrated and uneasy about this, she told him she didn't want to wait that long. In an attempt to force the issue and arrive at her goal sooner, she asked how long it would take if she worked harder, faster, and with more effort. "Ten to twelve years" was his reply.*

Unfortunately, this sports story is the rule, not the exception, with athletes. I experience this in my work constantly. It's important that you don't think of patience merely as the capacity to endure. Instead, embrace it as an opportunity to be at peace, and give yourself time to work toward your goal without time constraints as you enjoy the path of continual improvement. Remember the concept of *kaizen* in Part One: the slow, gradual process of consistent improvement. I like to ask athletes to recite this mantra when impatience is hindering their progress: Go Slower, Arrive Sooner.

Remember that in sports as in life, things occur not when you think they should, but when they are supposed to, when the time is right. There is a natural flow to all things. Think for a moment about the proverbial race between the tortoise and the hare. Through the inner kaizen-Buddha qualities of consistent, deliberate, steady slow movement, the tortoise arrives sooner than the faster yet more spastic and fatigued hare.

Perhaps the strongest virtue displayed by Buddha Tiger Woods is his palpable patience, winning or losing, up or down. He is mindful of the nature of the game, one of continual cycles as you go through some periods of not being at the top of your game. Tiger embraces golf's cyclical nature; he is a champion in high times as well as low. The Buddha knows the wisdom of steady, serene thoughts unaffected by the swings of life. For Tiger, the key to his success is patience, the calm and uncompromising [enduring] of inevitable change.

To help you get a sense of patience in action, consider a shift in your attitude as you contemplate the following about the ancient martial art Tai Ji (a.k.a. Tàijí quán or T'ai chi ch'üan) and invite others to join you:

> *Tai Ji practice is never in a rush to get someplace in the future. It is always in the present with the focus on the process. To experience this, wave your arms around the body slowly, feeling every detail of the joints throughout your arms clicking into action, softly propelling the rippling and curvaceous motion. We call this powerful, graceful motion "Cloud Hands." As you enjoy this Tai Ji way of waving your arms, you'll find yourself slowing down to savor this delicious and fun experience. You have now arrived at the place where you always want to be.*

The Competitive Buddha

Humility: The Buddha Bow

"When things are going well, be mindful of adversity. When prosperous, be mindful of poverty. When loved, be mindful of thoughtfulness. When respected, be mindful of humility."
—Buddhist Thought

In Buddhist cultures, bowing with the hands together is a simple gesture of modesty and humility. In so doing, we acknowledge the smallness of our own importance and our egos. This humble gesture, the traditional Buddha Bow, represents letting go of the importance of self while simultaneously appreciating and respecting all sentient beings. This is a core competitive Buddha principle: sincere reverence for life. Bowing is good for the soul as you recognize the unique importance of everyone as well as the smallness of the self.

When it comes to athletics, there are many opportunities for one to display humility. While the gesture of bowing is rarely observed, the opportunity to remain humble presents itself in various ways. For example, coaches and players can give praise and recognition to the defeated opponent in a post-game interview. "They are one of the best teams in the league. They deserved to win today as well," is a statement often spoken by humble athletes and coaches. The humility of knowing and expressing that you might win today but lose to the same team tomorrow keeps things in perspective.

Buddhist thought reminds us that a posture of humble heart and genuine respect will bring blessings from all directions. Humility, in sports and in all other arenas of life, is all about giving,—giving credit to others because without your opponents, teammates, coaches, parents, and other supportive people, you would not be where you are.

In Buddhist teachings, giving credit to others is called right speech, the avoidance of vain talk. Notice how those who boast of achievement have little merit. The need some people have to constantly prove themselves is exceedingly harmful, tiring, and detrimental to their mental and spiritual well-being. The warrior acts as if he has received nothing. I encourage you to feel secure in promoting others. Insecure people have a dire need to promote themselves, but you are more effective and appreciated when you demonstrate humility by focusing on the greatness of others.

In competition, there is always the risk of being too self-involved, or even smitten with your own prowess. The code of the competitive Buddha states that the more effort you expend in looking good, the further you separate yourself from your heart; excessively self-absorbed behavior creates inner battles, engendering much self-doubt. Be proud of your achievements, cherish your well-deserved recognition, celebrate your efforts, yet focus on others' accomplishments as well, giving recognition to the greatness of those around you. Notice how when you give praise to others, you feel good and they do as well. This creates an environment for others to sing your praises.

It's important for me to acknowledge that I am the result of all I've been given from others, gifts made possible through their lovingkindness. I am frequently known to admit that any wisdom I have accrued is the result of others helping me to go forward. Actually, I tell others that I am simply the hole at the end of the flute and the breaths of others wiser than myself come through me to you.

Think about this as you go about your day: In what ways can you display humility today? Here's a hint suggested by C.S. Lewis: "Humility is not thinking less of yourself; it's thinking about yourself less."

Further insight into the importance of the Buddhist virtue of humility as it relates to sports is found in the approach displayed by John Wooden, former coach of the UCLA Bruins; he often says that when his team wins, it is their doing; when they lose, it is his responsibility.

This is not to say that you cannot be proud of your team's or your own achievements. Cherish the moment of recognition of victory. Celebrate your efforts while remaining aware that bragging and self-aggrandizement are the patterns of insecure coaches who need to promote themselves, yet find it difficult to live up to this inflated image.

To secure honor and glory, give recognition to the greatness of those around you. Notice without expectation how others on your team, on your staff, or in your home, as well as your opponents, return the gesture. Learning lessons of humility will help you to become a better coach and person in every aspect of life. There's no need for you to do anything to make others become aware of your greatness. That will happen by itself. When you really think about it, people are usually uncomfortable around those who brag or boast. Have you ever noticed how your unsolicited retelling of your accomplishments, achievements, or advantages tends to be somewhat offensive and can even end up turning others against you? On the other hand, if others seem curious, you shouldn't hesitate to answer their questions and give them information about yourself that could further the conversation. Look for opportunities when you can sincerely affirm yourself and others.

The ancient book of Chinese wisdom, the *Tao Te Ching*, has some profound words regarding humility:

"Do not boast overly.
Keep the jade and treasures reserved within the bosom.
A posture of humble heart will bring blessings from all directions."

Present: The Fierce Urgency of Now

"The secret of health for both mind and body is not to mourn
for the past, worry about the future, or anticipate troubles,
but to live in the present moment wisely and earnestly."

—Buddhist Thought

For today's athlete, to mourn the past is to harp on a mistake, a missed shot, a faulty defensive move. To worry about the future is to dwell on the possible outcome, results, and statistics. Living in the present moment is intentionally dwelling in what is happening now… What are you doing, how are you in the moment, and what is happening all around you?

To be the best Buddha athlete, you must learn to live in the present. In his classic book *The Way of Zen*, Alan Watts refers to what Western mystics call the Eternal Now, awareness of this one eternal moment. This means to park your attention on to what's going on without focusing on past regrets or future fears. According to Watts, "I have realized that the past and future are real illusions, that they exist in the present, which is what there is and all there is."

What I have recently learned (and this may help you, too) is if I am thinking of the future, I come back to the present by reminding myself that I am thinking *right now in the present* about the past and future and simply acknowledging that fact; then I continue to follow what's going on now. It might sound like this: "Oh, I'm thinking of the future in this present moment. What else am I doing now? What can I think about now that will keep me in this precious moment?"

This is what athletes like Tiger Woods or Steph Curry or Megan Rapinoe do so well. And like these icons, we can all come back to the "now." Kobe was a true Buddha in his ability to be present most of the time on the court.

A competitive Buddha approach includes the awareness that in all physical activity, you must be focused in the here and now to experience mastery. What we all need to know is that being in the now is pure joy and satisfaction. Alan Watts points out that you don't dance to get to the other side of the floor; you don't sing to get to the end of the song. Neither should you work out, train, run, swim, bike, or do your job just to get it done. Focus on the joy of the process—minute by minute, day by day. Again, Kobe was brilliant at this, as he was with so many of these values. He didn't play to get to the end of the game or season.

To help you focus in this way, direct your attention to all the wonderful things going on inside you as you play. Feel the blood flow through the arterial pathways. Remind yourself of all the little things you must do now. Focus your eyes only on what you are doing: the ball, stick, field, weights—or the book you are writing. Choose a good visual target. Fill your ears with words of encouragement and positive expressions. If possible, listen to music that facilitates concentration in the moment. Or think about the runner who took all the numbers and hands off the face of his watch and wrote one word: *now*! Wow! He had the correct time, every second of every day. Try to season your life as if you were going to live forever, yet act as if this is your last day on earth. Carpe diem: 'Seize the day.' In the words of Dr. Martin Luther King, Jr., feel *"the fierce urgency of now."*

By the way, I must tell you that as I wrote this book, every minute of the journey included the music of R. Carlos Nakai playing Native American flute on my Spotify playlist. It puts me into a totally creative, relaxed and present state.

Gratitude: Counting
Your Blessings

"Acknowledging the good that you already have in
your life is the foundation of all abundance."
—Eckhart Tolle

"You have no cause for anything but gratitude and joy."
—Buddhist Thought

According to Buddhist thought, gratitude is one of the best
practices for living every day. It is closely connected to the
concept of mindfulness. Practicing gratitude helps us all to be
more aware of our connection to our lives and how we are a
small part of a larger purpose. It liberates us from the worry,
endless desires, and suffering caused by focusing on what we
lack. Gratitude is the key to personal happiness and joy. It
helps you to change fear into faith and faith into courage. It
brings about feelings of love, compassion, and connection. It is
life-changing.

Buddhist thought encourages us to be mindful of all the
good that is in our lives, including all we've been given by our
parents, friends, and teachers, and to do it intentionally, to
cultivate it rather than just letting it happen randomly. It is a
simple daily practice of what I call "counting your blessings."

How relevant is this concept to the world of sport? Many
athletes complain about what they don't have or what they're
not getting rather than paying attention to what they have been
given. The Buddha athlete does not dwell on lack of playing
time, poor stats, or little or no recognition. Rather, the focus of
the mindful athlete is on feeling well, healthy, and strong and
noticing all the fortunate opportunities given. There are a lot

The Competitive Buddha

of positives worth remarking on, like friendship, community, growth, development, and the joy and fun of being able to be part of a team—something bigger than personal gain or loss. It has become well-known that gratitude is good for athletics: Gratitude tops negativity as it rewires your brain, eliminates stress, improves self-esteem, and raises levels of performance.

What I notice working with athletes over several decades is how most of the truly great ones are filled with gratitude, one of the foundational strengths of the Mamba Mentality. The teams that perform at their very best are grateful. They are also very happy and joyful, states of mind that translate into better performance. My friend Brother David Steindl-Rast, a Benedictine monk, reminds me that the root of joy is gratefulness… It is not joy that makes us grateful; it is gratitude that makes us joyful.

In the world of sports, we fall into the trap of what's missing; we're not big enough, strong enough, talented enough, good enough…enough already! It's easier to think about scarcity rather than focusing on being grateful for what we have. To help with this, I recommend expressing appreciation as a daily practice. For five minutes each day, focus on your gratitude for what you have been given—for all of your blessings. Then go about the rest of your day making everything you do a reflection of these gifts.

Gratitude is the process of becoming mindful of what is genuinely important and holding that feeling in your heart. What's important to you, what you appreciate, can change each day depending upon what comes your way. For me, certain items are more constant, as in this gratitude statement I wrote: "I am grateful for my family, my life partner, my ability to make a difference in the lives of others through my writing and work, my healthy body, my comfortable home, my mental clarity, my sense of humor…" and so on. Each day new items get added to the list.

Here's an exercise that I practice regularly. I do this before getting out of bed, and it has the power to transform my days and impact everything I am doing as well as my state of being. Give this a shot, and be sure to include everything that's good and special about your life.

- Make a list of five or more items that make you feel grateful.

- Go over the list and get connected to how these make you feel: calm, peaceful, loving, fortunate, blessed…all feelings of gratitude.

- Take in one deep, slow breath through your nose. And as you do, take in this feeling of gratefulness. As you bring this feeling in to surround your heart, hold your breath for four seconds, and then slowly release it.

- Repeat this deep breathing three times.

- Notice how relaxed and peaceful you feel. Now go about the rest of the day and make everything a reflection of what you've been given. In other words, give back.

Notice the difference in how you perform. The ordinary will become extraordinary. This alignment with your heart will give you a broader, richer, more meaningful perspective on all the mundane realities of sports as well as in life.

Here is more wisdom from Brother David:

> Look closely and you will find that people are happy because they are grateful… Everything is a gift. The degree to which we are awake to this truth is a measure of our gratefulness, and gratefulness is a measure of our aliveness… We are never more than one grateful thought away from peace of heart.

Having gratitude is an attitude…An "attitude of gratitude" contributes to your overall health and has a profound impact on masterful performance as you go from "grateful to great."

Simplicity: Less Is More

"If you endeavor to embrace the Way through much learning, the Way will not be understood. If you observe the Way with simplicity of heart, great indeed is the Way."

—Buddhist Thought

We are all drowning in a sea of information. There is too much to learn, too much to know. This is complicating our way. The Buddha asks us to notice the great way of simplicity; when we do, greater happiness will be ours. It has been said that the Buddha left all of his wealth behind to simply be in nature.

The world of athletics is becoming extremely complex, and we could learn a more simple, happier way from the Buddha. From the time children are five years old, family life can be disrupted by an unreasonable and demanding schedule of practices, sporting events, and competitions requiring much travel at exorbitant costs, all in the hope that our kids will qualify to catch the next train to Stanford. It continues into high school and beyond. Whatever happened to the simpler days of just playing in the sandbox? Sports are out of control, and one must wonder, are we any better off because of it? Think about all the attendant technological advances: watches, heart-rate monitors, energy bars, replacement drinks, exercise machines. Clearly much is gained, yet so much is lost. Whatever happened to listening to your body for appropriate feedback? Ethiopian Abebe Bikila won an Olympic gold medal in the marathon running barefoot. No high-tech shoes or digital timepiece for him; he simply ran. Complex gadgetry can create distraction, anxiety, and tension, hindering performance.

Take a close look at your exercise and sports agenda. Think about ways in which you can seriously create change toward a more simplified program. What's essential and what's not? Do you really need all that equipment? Will having those expensive running shoes really help you to run up that hill more quickly? If so, is it necessary to run so quickly? Do you really need to jump into your car and drive thirty minutes each day to an exercise gym when you might be able to gain the same benefits by lifting weights at home, using the travel time saved for reading or meditation? For some athletes and exercise buffs, portable heart monitors are useful and worth having, an integral aspect of their training; for others, they are superfluous gear of little value. How do you feel about this?

As you begin to feel the numerous benefits from a shift to a simpler consciousness about your physical world, you may become motivated to do the same in other aspects of your life. Take a look at your environment, your diet, your relationships, your career, and your possessions. What can you shed to create a less complicated lifestyle? By noticing this, you will begin to manifest increased happiness in your life by following the less is more approach: a simple meal, a simple day, a simple home. There's less to worry about; it hardly matters when your no-frills ten-year-old car gets scratched in a parking lot. For some, a computer is essential; for others, it's an expensive toy they can do without.

Creating simplicity in your complex world is not easy. It requires rethinking priorities and the willingness to empty your pockets to fill your soul. Taking a cut in salary could mean more hours with the family, quality time with your hobbies, and less upheaval, even if there's less money left over at the end of the month. Simplifying requires coming to terms with a deeper spiritual question: "How much is enough?" As opposed to, "How much can I get?" Perhaps it means learning how to live simply in order to simply live.

Simplicity is liberating. It helps you to focus only on that which really matters. Mastery is experienced during times of pure, unadulterated simplicity. Perhaps the greatest sophistication in life is when we can embrace the competitive Buddha sports way: Less is more.

Faith: Having Belief, Not Fear

"When your faith becomes stronger than fear,
Then your dreams can become a reality."
—Buddhist Thought

"On a long journey of human life,
Faith is the best companion."
—Buddhist Thought

Like the Buddha, when I speak of faith, I speak about belief and confidence in oneself. I'm talking about the essence of the Mamba Mind and how Kobe's confidence was based in his belief that he could manifest his best most of the time. To have confidence in ourselves, we must develop the awareness that we have Buddha nature within us right now—and faith that we can act and behave according to the Noble Eightfold Path (see Part Three). This notion is affirmed by the insightful, empowering words of Buddhist master Hakuin, who says in "The Song of Zazen," "Sentient beings are primarily all Buddhas." He asks that we have faith in the thought that each one of us is a Buddha. Without this faith and essential spiritual self-confidence, we wind up drifting along in a confused state of fear, afraid to journey inward while being controlled by sources outside of ourselves. We lose all self-confidence in our ability to choose and make good decisions. We fail to trust that the wise Buddha is already present within. The true nature of our reality is dependent upon only that which resides on the inside.

How does this relate to Buddha Sports? To begin with, in so much of athletic performance, anxiety and fear is caused by external factors—past mistakes and possible future losses, to name two. Fear is the biggest obstacle to mastery and success; I call it a cancer of the athletic soul. It weakens you, causing you to be tight, tense, and tentative. The cure for this cancer is faith—faith that you have the Buddha mastery strategies deep within, faith in your coaches and the system, and faith in your team. It is a faith not in outcome, but in all the little things you can control, such as solid defense, work effort and ethic, attitude about competition, preparation, and all the competitive Buddha precepts outlined in this book. Knowing that you can have an influence in these ways will improve your confidence, trust, belief, and faith from within so that you will not be manipulated by external influences that cannot be controlled.

What I'm saying is to have faith that the Buddhist teachings included in this section are available to you and can be practiced daily. This is the way to strengthen your belief and weaken your fear. Here are how things work when you begin to manifest the Mamba "Beginner's Mind."

If your mind believes "I can't," you will sabotage your work efforts. You won't do what's required to be in a state of mastery. But when you shift your mind's approach towards the Buddha Brain and Mamba Beginner's Mind, you believe, "I can," and you follow paths of behavior and thought that help ensure that mastery is possible. The psychology of this type of thinking includes the mindsets of hope, motivation, commitment, confidence, courage, concentration, excitement, and observation.

It takes work to renounce your restrictive beliefs about what you can and can't do in sport. Your power as a Buddha athlete starts with awareness that you have unlimited potential once you align yourself with the belief "I can." Remember that acting "as if" you can achieve something is self-direction, not self-deception. It places you on the path of mastery. As you forge ahead, you can learn from your setbacks and mistakes. Hard opinions about yourself distort the truth about your potential. Be flexible in your beliefs: Rigidity will block your growth.

When you function with a flexible Mamba Mind, you access a clear vision and a nonjudgmental mental state that gives you faith and belief. Then what's needed is to simply "act as if" and focus your behavior on all the ways of Buddha and Mamba Sports, a process-oriented approach with the wisdom of a diligent work ethic.

Most athletes at all levels of play from the recreational enthusiast up to the professional end up utilizing far less than half of their potential. Why should you believe anything other than "I can"? Approach each free throw, putt, pitch, fly ball, pass, stroke, spike, or technical maneuver with a positive inner belief of *yes*—act "as if," and activate your concentration, your belief, and your faith in the Buddha within, in the Mamba Mind path of mastery.

William James, the great American philosopher, once said that the greatest discovery of his generation was that, "Human beings, by changing the inner beliefs of their minds, can change the outer aspects of their lives." And Buddhist teaching reminds us that if you're facing in the right direction, all you need to do is keep on walking that path. This is exactly what the Mamba Mentality is all about, showing how changing inner beliefs can change outer aspects of life.

Balance: The Buddhist Middle Way

"Maintain a state of balance between physical acts and inner
serenity, like a lute whose strings are finely tuned."
—Buddhist Thought

Buddhist teaching talks about the "Middle Way." It is the
understanding of attaining a practical life, by avoiding the
extremes of self-indulgence and self-denial. It is this Middle
Way that can help all of us reach enlightenment. Buddhism
teaches that if we live in a moderate way, many of the problems
of the world, such as poverty, homelessness, and hunger, could
be minimized, if not avoided completely. Taking the Middle
Way can lead to wisdom, insight, and calmness as you become
free of suffering; it is the way to peace and freedom in this very
life. The middle path brings freedom. It is about being mindful
and letting things take their natural course (see Epilogue).
To become extreme in one area of life causes you to neglect
something else.

Reaching our highest potential and personal mastery always
comes through balance, not extremes. The great philosopher
Aristotle told us, "All things in moderation." Today's world
of fitness and sports has become synonymous with the
word "extreme." The influence of triathletes, body builders,
ultrarunners, and other extreme athletes on sports culture, while
inspiring, make it more difficult to find balance, the ultimate
key to achieving best results. There needs to be a balance, a
middle place where attention is given to body, mind, and spirit
if you are to reach your full human potential. It is, in Buddhist
language, the right view of life as you transcend and reconcile
the extremes of nature.

This is the age of specialization, especially with youth sports. The Buddhist idea of the Middle Way has traditionally been ignored by many young as well as older athletes.

In youth sports, you find youngsters completely out of balance in their entire lives, in particular, imbalanced by their obsession of competing in one sport only for the entire year. Parents fear that their precious child will miss out on scholarship opportunities if they don't log thousands of hours with a sport. As a parent of four children who diversified their sports experiences, I feel strongly that generalization and diversifying athletic pursuits leads to healthier, happier, better prepared kids. I have been advised over the years by so many professional athletes that the best way to help your kids is to encourage their participation in a variety of sports. I grew up in a neighborhood where all of us played different sports, often all on the same summer day. Five of these friends went on to play professionally, and the rest of us competed at the national level. To this day, I run, bike, hike, and visit the gym. In my bestseller *Let Them Play*, I have a whole section on creating balance in your kids' lives called *Specialization or Diversification?*

For me, balance is created every day by being aware of what's on my list of ongoing to-do items. If I manage to accomplish seven of them, I feel my life has balance. The ten items are: run or walk, eat well, meditate, read, affirm others, perform one random act of kindness, help others to feel important and valued, do some strength training, feel grateful, and write. Minimum amount of time expended on each is five minutes. Using that as a guide, I could actually complete all ten in under three hours, assuming I run for an hour. All of these fit comfortably around my usual seven-hour work day. There is time if you truly wish to balance life.

I notice how more and more, we are becoming aware of a Middle Way and changing our lives, and for good reason. In his New Your Times bestseller *Range*, David Epstein points out how research that's been done on the world's top performers in sports and other arenas of life shows that early specialization is becoming the exception, not the rule. The generalists are now being found to be victorious in an overspecialized, out of balance world. What we had believed to be true for years is now being proven wrong.

The effects of an overall lack of balance on one's life are easily understood by observing the reactions of Olympic athletes at the completion of their long, arduous journey toward the gold. Rewarding as a prizewinning outcome may be, how does the intense, narrowly focused lifestyle affect the development of these stars, particularly the younger ones? In a recent Olympiad, one of the champion swimmers was asked, "Where do you go from here?" The response was instantaneous: "Far away from pools." He vowed to avoid swimming in a pool for the next two years. He proceeded to relate how much had been sacrificed on his road to fame and intimated that it might not have been worth it. He felt that the lack of balance in his life had contributed to his feelings of stress, confusion, distraction, fatigue, and burnout; yet because of this narrow focus, he was able to reach great heights.

As an achiever myself, I have often experienced the absence of this balanced Buddha way. There have been periods when I've been obsessed with competitive running to the exclusion of everything else. I also have at times become so self-absorbed in my work that I ignored my family and friends. And then there have been moments in which I would just play, day after day, and do a good job at it. Other aspects of my reality, however, were put on hold. I "succeeded" at what I did, yet I knew something was lost in the process. I still felt a void—something was missing. My lopsided, asymmetrical existence was not as fulfilling as I thought it would be. I am presently creating a balance in my life between body, mind, and emotions, and it feels terrific. Best of all, I've learned that I can still be good at what I do; *balance and excellence are compatible partners.* Actually, I believe that with balance, excellence is more attainable. Those who seem to do the best in their field— the people I most admire—are those who have established a wonderful "evenness" to their personal, social, home, and community lives.

This brings us to another competitive Buddha principle, one that if followed, will enhance the opportunities for personal joy and happiness. It states: *The extent of one's fulfillment in life is the direct result of the balance created between the physical, mental, and emotional-spiritual selves.* Failure to attend to all components creates a void that will restrain total wellness and joy. Concentrating only on any one in particular produces an extreme condition, as well as imbalance with the way of nature. By following the teachings of Buddha, extremes can be avoided while you gain personal power through moderation. Buddha Sports can assist you in your attempts to become aware of extremes and restore the balance. Buddha is the balance; you just need to notice that.

The process of creating balance in life is no different from the way one balances a diet. Good nutrition means that the body is presented with the right combination of carbohydrates, fats, and proteins, with the amounts varying depending on the individual's needs. So it is with life. You function more effectively and experience greater overall wellness when balance is established between the *body, mind,* and *spirit.* As with a diet, such synchronicity is possible only when you keep a constant vigil; you must always notice other patterns you follow and correct for error when drifting off course.

Being successful in finding and maintaining the balance is all about time management. Many people believe there isn't enough time to "do it all." There is plenty of time; you just have to learn to use it more efficiently.

Perhaps a more precise word besides balance that I could use to talk about the Middle Way is the idea of *equanimity*. I love this word and how it encompasses the entire spectrum of the Middle Way. Buddhist thought addresses this concept when it relates how "*The sage, when touched by happiness and then by suffering, shows no sign of being elated or depressed,*" a state of complete equanimity.

And I will leave you with this provocative thought by the German author Goethe: "*So divinely is the world organized that every one of us, in our place and time, is in balance with everything else.*"

Part Three

NOBLE MINDFUL LEADERSHIP

The Buddha Heart for Transformative Coaching

"Go forth, O monks, on your wanderings, for the good of
the many, for the happiness of the many, out of compassion
of the world. O monks, proclaim the Dharma, which is
good at the beginning, at the middle, and at the end."
—Buddhist Thought

This Buddha message is emblematic of what Buddha himself
thought to be good noble mindful leadership. According to
Buddhism, the path of such effective leadership is to become a
mindful leader with an open heart by practicing mindfulness
meditation. (See Mindfulness section below in this part.) The

key factor in one's successful involvement as a leader is to cultivate love and compassion for others.

Most of us could easily say that the Buddha was one of the most important, empowering, and influential leaders in the history of the world. He was a transformative leader with a strong leadership purpose: leading others out of suffering. He was able to accomplish this through his noble teachings and his service to others. By "Noble," the Buddha meant something that has worth for all people. His leadership strategy was to transform humanity by cultivating a mindful noble heart, one of love, friendship, courage, peace, trust, tolerance, loyalty, humor, patience, vulnerability, accountability, vision, and other heart driven virtues. He was the quintessential role model of the awakened leader.

While researching Buddhism and leadership, I came across an eloquent piece from the May 2016 issue of *The Nation* (Thailand) called "The Buddha Concept of Leadership" by Chandima Wijebandara. According to him, the most unique feature of Buddha's leadership was how "he never gave the impression to his followers that he was imposing leadership on them." He hoped to convey leadership in a subtle and humble way. The Buddha was friendly, which made him very approachable. Such leadership is built on trust, and gaining others' trust demands a high degree of moral integrity. This is why I called this part of the book "Awakening the Buddha Heart," a heart that dictates your words and actions, making you the ideal role model to emulate. With such moral integrity, followers will go the distance and then go on to become leader mentors of mindful spiritual leadership for their subsequent followers. And, ultimately, they will say they did it themselves.

Notice how the bumblebee extracts honey from flowers without destroying the color or fragrance of the flower.

The Competitive Buddha

So it is with the Buddha-like leader, who serves humanity while avoiding doing harm or hurting others, keeping the environment safe and secure. Only then will followers feel free to develop their full human capacity.

Here we are, 2,500 years since Buddha lived, with an even greater need of good, mindful spiritual leadership in athletics, as well as the kind of sports culture where coaches can develop the capacity to do no harm to their sports team and athletes. Mindful coaches are transformational leaders, not transactional; they are leaders who are attentive to the needs of athletes, helping them to reach their full potential and achieve a greater sense of self-actualization as the athletes, too, become mindful leaders for others. In the eloquent words of Chandi, "A sign of a good leader is not how many followers you have, but how many leaders you create." The teachings of the Buddha help in this regard. In fact, this section of the book as well as the previous section express truths of the Buddha to inspire and awaken leadership within as well as enabling mastery, all of which promotes a joyful athletic coaching experience. To be successful, today's coach in athletics needs to demonstrate a noble heart, which is what all aspects of this book address either directly or by implication. This is accomplished by the cultivation of a Buddha approach to leadership, one that influences one to right thoughts, speech, and action (see "The Noble Eightfold Traits of Mindful Leaders" near the end of Part 3), expressing the qualities of a mindful, effective leader, which are presented in this part of the book.

Awakening the
Relationship Dance

"Regard your athletes as your children, and they may follow wherever you lead. Look upon them as your beloved sons and daughters, and they will stand by you until death."

—Sun-Tzu, *The Art of War*

For the past few decades, I have honed my leadership wisdom, learning from the best of the best in the coaching world, including Dean Smith, Steve Kerr, Pete Carroll, Phil Jackson, Anson Dorrance, Bill Walsh, John Wooden, Cindy Timchal, Pat Summitt, and Tara VanDerveer, to name a few. What I notice is how much they honor, respect, and promote leadership styles very similar to what is taught by the Buddha, bringing a more heart filled approach to their coaching. These coaches, like the Buddha, are fiercely authentic, vulnerable, courageous risk takers; they are pensive listeners, flexible, adaptable, spiritually awake, and lead balanced lives. They lead by example, not by coercion.

Another such coach is Quin Snyder, head coach of the NBA Utah Jazz. On a recent Way of Champions podcast, we were conversing about how Quin is the master of the relationship game with how he's able to get his athletes to work hard, be loyal, and go the distance in practice and games alike. We affirmed his talents in this aspect of leadership. That night, his team was competing in a very tough game against the Boston Celtics in Boston. The Jazz were outstanding in their victory. The next morning, I received an interesting text from Quin: "I think the uplifting podcast spilled over to our team." Yes, it did, I replied. When we are reminded about the ingredients of a healthy relationship game, we tend to bring these traits to our work with those we lead and coach.

Over time, I have been witness to a virtual sea change, a huge paradigm shift taking place in the profession of coaching; athletes are demanding positive relationship change with their leaders. Such a historic shift tells me that those being coached are seeking a change of heart from those doing the coaching towards a more dynamic multifaceted approach. While athletes are still interested in the necessity of developing and learning the essential skills, tactics, and strategies of their sport, they also seem to desire being taught this knowledge in environments that are steeped in respect, trust, love, compassion, and integrity. In other words, while they care about what you know as their coach (the X's and O's), they also want to know that you care (inspiration and empowerment). In a sense, they are asking their leaders to "dance" with a mindful noble heart. Coaches who are successful in sport are beginning to realize that they need to win the "relationship game," and that when that happens, the athletic game takes care of itself. What they are discovering is that, much like the Buddha path, coaching is ultimately a path of the heart, a relationship dance between athlete and coach. For the coach, there is a corresponding inward dance between teaching the athletes skill sets for optimal performance and supporting them in developing wisdom and insight.

To be a truly mindful Buddha coach, mentor, leader, and teacher, you too must be a good student and learn what needs to be known from your student (the athlete) in order to teach them what they must learn. In this dancing relationship, each individual is interdependent—forming a bond of equal fulfillment, love, and respect in a harmonious atmosphere of openness, communication, and loyalty. Each person involved in this mutually beneficial dance genuinely experiences the gifts each side has to offer. This fluid, rhythmic, flowing, and dancing union between coach and athlete, serving and sharing together for the greater good of all, is an extraordinary process to behold. It is the cornerstone of the awakened noble heart leader. True learning and development take place in all arenas of life when giving and receiving have become everyday actions for each member of the relationship. When you feel relevant, important, valued, respected, and empowered, you will go the distance and manifest loyalty and mental strength.

Extraordinary Buddha leadership and coaching involves the coach's devoting his or her time and energy to performance management, strategic planning, and a myriad of other "X's and O's" type preparatory exercises. While these aspects of leadership are absolutely essential to the coaching function, there is also the need for a union that enables you to inspire and empower those being led. Herein lies the essence of mindful Buddha leadership.

The challenge at this point is for all of us to discover ways to create safe environments and develop mindful relationships with heart; that's where we as leaders can perfect the Buddha qualities of love, inspiration, compassion, respect, understanding, and integrity while concurrently helping each athlete to develop the skill sets necessary to perform the tasks at hand. When we influence our athletes in this way, they feel valued, and they perform more optimally in an encouraging environment free of fear and intimidation. With an increase of love, compassion, and spirituality, people become happy, trust and respect deepen, and results and outcomes are greatly enhanced. Simply stated, when we develop relationships like this, those we lead are more joyful, cooperative, and happy and therefore work harder; when anyone works harder, results and outcomes usually improve.

Additionally, athletes in such environments will begin to prepare, practice, play, compete, and live with heart themselves. Your coaching becomes the model used by all those under your guidance for their own personal leadership on and off the field.

The mindful Buddha coach leads by example and attitude. The Buddhist way is one of coaching by guiding rather than forcing others to comply, since coercion builds resentment and rebellion; better to create environments of loyalty, trust, respect, and cooperation where resistance and counterforce are virtually eliminated, while instilling a strong sense of personal power in those you lead. You will discover that by being such a heart-directed leader, you will empower others and simultaneously gain power yourself. Like electricity, the more energy and love you conduct, the more you receive. In truth, you never need to display power. Others just feel and respect it because an extraordinary leader radiates and emanates personal power. The principles, wisdom, and overall lessons of the Buddha will guide you to develop a more athlete-centered approach for those under your guidance, thus helping you to master the art of highly effective, enlightened, and extraordinary leadership.

The following are several specific examples of what mindful Buddha leaders do to create and cultivate a heart-directed culture:

- Spark the flames of enthusiasm, excitement, and inspiration that flicker in all athletes

- Encourage you to win the inner battles for success in all of life

- Create environments that are emotionally safe, without blame and judgment

- Enable you to realize your full, expansive capacity in sports and life

- Nurture team cohesion, harmony, and unity of purpose: one heart, one soul, one goal

- Gain the dedication, trust, loyalty, love, and appreciation of all those you lead

- Communicate so that they will listen to you and you to them

- Permit risk and help you learn the lessons of failure for sport and life

- Model powerful humanistic styles of leadership

- Resolve conflict more peacefully and effectively

- Create more joy, happiness, and fulfillment for athletes, helping them to perform at higher levels

- Cultivate independence, interdependence, and confidence in those you lead

- Encourage athletes to turn to the staff and team in times of crisis, rather than to outsiders or drugs

- Nurture self-esteem in others and in yourself

- Be respectful and sensitive to athletes' needs

To lead your athletes in the right direction and make a penetrating positive impact on their spirits, fight for and win their hearts in a profound way using this Buddha wisdom and serve them well. Gandhi phrased it in this simple way:

> **"I suppose leadership at one time meant muscles;
> but today it means getting along with people."**

As I mentioned before, the Buddha way is the guiding mindset where the leader guides, not directs, athletes to become the best version of themselves. Guidance without excessive control opens the doors of mastery. Setting generous boundaries will encourage others to follow your system yet feel free to explore personal potential. This reminds me of the ancient question: How does the farmer control the cows? By moving the fences back.

Control blocks growth, vision, creativity, and ultimately mastery. The Buddha way is to let the best happen in an environment of connection, caring, and love. Coaches who let go of excessive control are usually those who are secure within themselves. In the words of the wise Taoist teacher Confucius, a great leader "guides others and does not pull them along; urges them to go forward, yet refuses to take them to the place." To be a more mindful coach, try the following ways to awaken your Buddha heart for transformative leadership.

- Be open to listening to criticism from others, particularly if it is the opinion of the majority. As a coach, corporate executive, or head of a household, show others your openness to feedback by asking them periodically (especially during times of tension and disharmony) to respond in writing to this question: "If you were in charge and had complete freedom to handle things your way, what would you do and how would you do it?" They should respond to this question anonymously in order to ensure honest and truthful responses. They will respect and admire you for this, especially if you initiate positive change based on their suggestions and criticisms.

- Create an open, positive environment using the coaching qualities from the next section (on the Noble Eightfold Path), an environment where all feel accepted, respected, and able to grow as individuals. Be fair; show no favoritism to the "stars." For example, all athletes or members of the team should work equally hard. With regard to guidelines for team or group conduct, be consistent. Team members appreciate behavior boundaries, which foster a sense of security. But within that structure, be sure to give them the freedom to develop and be themselves.

- Before you criticize those you lead, first look for ways to give them credit. This too is taken from the Buddhist truths outlined in the following section on the Noble Eightfold Path. For example, you can say, "Sonia, I love the way you always hustle. Now, if you want to kick it up a notch, use your hands like this, and shuffle your feet at the same time." By the time you criticize her arms and footwork, she is ready to listen, knowing you have acknowledged her work ethic. Be sure to provide concrete, specific data for your critique. Avoid gross generalizations such as "you always" or "you never." Search for ways that you, together with the athlete, coworker, or family member, can address the problem. Suggestions coming from them will hold more weight, and compliance will come more easily. When feasible, don't criticize during a performance. Your comments will be more effective if you wait and introduce them after practice session or on the next day.

- As a coach or team leader, you need to understand that your position is only as strong and secure as you make your athletes feel. The players or workers can make you or break you.

- If you demonstrate a sincere willingness to be Buddha-like and help and serve others, they will approach you for advice and guidance. If you are willing to listen to others, they will be attracted to you and partake in a wonderful exchange of ideas. The Buddha considered himself a servant. and today, there is a whole movement about servant leadership (the next section: Servant Leader of Warriors).

The Competitive Buddha

- Avoid manipulation at all costs. As a leadership style, it creates anger, resentment, and loss of respect on the part of those it's used against. Power plays, trying to exert your position over others, and being "the boss" are forms of manipulation that create environments of distrust and suspicion. Motivation, morale, and team spirit diminish with the use of such tactics.

- Remember the Golden Rule of Buddhism: "Hurt not others with that which pains yourself." If you follow this rule, your problems will be minimized. Harshness gets you nowhere, why use it? When you use the Buddha approach of lovingkindness, you win their hearts and cooperation, which is what you really want and deserve.

- Create emotionally safe environments where setbacks, mistakes, errors, and failures are permissible. In this way, people will take risks to explore their personal levels of mastery without fear of criticism, judgment, or penalty.

Awakening to the Buddha heart with your coaching will be transformative for you as well as your athletes. It will help you to begin to be more open, trusting, vulnerable, confident, and aware that we are part of a larger game—one greater than the one we coach. With the Buddha by your side, athletics becomes a conduit for inner growth, change, and expansion for those we coach, helping them to experience something beyond the ordinary. This is when we all live, play, coach, and compete in alignment with our hearts, the place where we live the Buddha dream of being a better version of ourselves each and every day. It is a sacred space of greater meaning, more joy, and masterful performance, meeting many of your physical, mental, emotional, and spiritual needs.

Servant Leader of Warriors

"Servant leadership is more than a concept, it's a fact. Any great leader will see herself or himself as a servant of that group."

—M. Scott Peck, author

Now that you have been awakened to the relationship dance, it's time to explore the notion of servant leadership, first coined by Dr. Robert Greenleaf in 1970 when he wrote his groundbreaking piece titled "The Servant Leader." In this article, he states how the good leader is a servant first.

Yet interestingly, the roots of this modern-day concept were planted long ago in the ancient philosophies of Taoist and Buddhist thought. In the *Tao Te Ching*, perhaps one of the first books ever written on leadership, Lao-tzu talks about how great servant leaders enable followers to say "we did it ourselves" in the cooperation and collaborative process of working together to grow as leaders.

I bring attention now to the ancient concept of the Samurai leader warrior in service. The word *samurai* in Japanese means 'one who attends or serves.' In this sense, the ideal coach or leader is akin to the Samurai, one who serves and leads with heart. Service is not about servitude or catering to all the wishes of those you lead. It is about valuing those you lead and adding worth to their lives. As a servant coach, you are in charge and oversee the big picture, but you offer your efforts in service to providing an honorable and humble environment for all to reach their potential.

As a Native American member of the Onondaga nation, Faithkeeper and Chief Oren Lyons, speaking in an interview called "Leadership Imperative," says that the purpose of leadership is to serve others. It appears that the most effective

The Competitive Buddha

leaders examine their hearts and ask themselves this question: Am I here to serve or to be served? Obviously, it's to serve. Therefore, the most important question that a service-oriented leader and coach needs to ask is, "How can I best serve you?" When you pay attention to the answer to this simple query, those you lead will experience a heightened sense of self; and as a result, you gain more power, not *over* people, but the power to influence them and help facilitate change and growth for all involved in a dynamic dance of positive interaction. This is why we say, "To serve is to lead."

Buddhist thought expounds the idea of selfless servant leaders who embody profound compassion and wisdom in their unrelenting effort to promote the growth of other mindful leaders with an open heart. The Buddhist servant leadership mission is to transform the relationship between leader and follower through conscious choice, giving rise to genuine caring and common interest in a shared vision. That vision of leadership is parallel with the code of the Samurai (literally one who serves), which included the following behavior:

- Willingness to admit mistakes and use them to better oneself
- Adhering to a set of personal values and being the change you want to see
- Mediating conflict in a cooperative way
- Picking up the slack when needed
- Acknowledging all opinions
- Listening
- Performing random acts of kindness
- Holding oneself to a higher standard
- Supporting those you lead during the hard times

- Committing to the growth of others
- Being patient and understanding
- Being demanding out of love for the benefit of others' growth
- Catching those you lead doing something right

While implementing these Buddha servant leader behaviors, make sure that your followers' highest priorities and needs are being served. Help them to grow as people—to become leaders in their own right. In this model of servant leadership, you share power and put the needs of the team first. Your actions in service inspire and empower others to dream, learn, and expand their horizons. Servant leaders invite others in with heart to work side-by-side with them rather than from above.

The truth that good leaders must become good servants is best exemplified by head coaches Phil Jackson, Pete Carroll, Tara VanDerveer, Gregg Popovich, Cindy Timchall, and Quin Snyder. Then there is Steve Kerr, whom I mentioned in the previous section. Steve believes in this concept and felt honored by the title I used for this section.

As the title to this section intimates, Steve is the *servant leader of warriors.* Like a true servant, Steve leads his athletes by walking behind them, inspiring and empowering them to develop their full human potential, regardless of their tole on the team. In a recent podcast we did together, Steve told us how you never want to let the last athlete on the bench to feel unimportant, devalued, and disrespected. He talks about how he uses several of the Buddha servant behaviors above to motivate all his athletes to find their personal greatness as athletes and as human beings.

The question many have about coaching at this level is this: How do you get a cohort of wealthy athletes to selflessly give to the collective good of even a star-studded team? According to Kerr, you make everyone feel relevant and important as part of something greater than any one individual. This is an essential aspect of servant leadership. By being a humble servant coach... while still being demanding, he is able to manage egos, keep players engaged, and build a strong team culture embodying the servant leader approach.

While Steve seems to come to this coaching style naturally, he humbly gives credit to many of his coaching mentors who taught him the servant way, coaches like Lute Olson, and as already mentioned, Phil Jackson, Gregg Popovich, and Pete Carroll as well, among others. For all of us who desire to adopt a more of a service approach to leadership, the most important lesson that Steve learned from these masters was simple: Be true to your values, principles and ideas...be yourself. He believes, as do all great leaders, that these values must be shared and followed every day. Steve's values are deeply rooted in the competitive Buddha approach, values like joy, selflessness, competitiveness, and mindfulness.

As a true servant leader, Kerr is consciously aware of individual needs, concerns, and personalities and remains flexible to adjust his coaching to individual players; by so doing, he helps them to maintain their uniqueness while working together for the greater good of the team. The servant leader needs to give athletes the bandwidth to be themselves while still holding on to the overall mission of the organization.

And, as a true servant leader, Steve is able to control his own ego and remain humble as he listens to his athletes. He understands that he is not all-knowing and encourages athletes and staff to contribute to his process. Ultimately, the decision is his, but he seriously considers everyone's input.

As a servant leader, Steve has a high level of emotional intelligence. He is humble, empathetic, genuine, authentic, and vulnerable. Vulnerability in a leader correlates to a high level of functioning. While some view it as weakness, servant leader coaches understand it's a strength. All extraordinary leaders, by definition, realize the power of demonstrating vulnerability. Steve is not afraid to admit he made a mistake. He'll apologize to a player he has wronged and will not take anything personally.

Perhaps one of the most vital signs of a servant leader is willingness to listen to others. Coach Kerr will often ask for an athlete's input regardless of their role on the team, listen to their words, and implement the athlete's ideas if relevant to the team's mission. This open dialogue gains the trust and respect of the team. He connects with the guys so he can understand and empathize with their personal life situations. Steve knows there is more to life than basketball; he understands what matters in the lives of those he leads. He is the extraordinary *servant leader of warriors*, whose coaching philosophy has deep-rooted connections to the competitive Buddha way.

If your wish is to have others follow your coaching, perhaps the most crucial quality of leadership you can possess is the ability to think beyond self-interest. This is the Buddha servant style of guiding others to be self-reliant, which supports their growth in the long run. As servant leaders, our mission is simply to guide others to pathways for a greater, more meaningful experience in life. An athlete recently told me, "Jerry, it is widely known that Jesus was the quintessential servant leader. He was the lamb-like servant of the church."

The well-known Russian novelist Leo Tolstoy once said: "The sole purpose of life is to serve humanity. It is the honorable and right thing to do." And in the process, you become more respected, loved, and worthy as you enhance the lives of all as their servant leader.

The Way of Love in Coaching

"We will develop love, we will practice it, we
will make it both a way and a basis."
—Buddhist Thought

This is the perfect time to segue from the concept of being
a servant leader to what extraordinary coaches believe is the
greatest leadership success strategy ever. These icons have
discovered the futility of the love of power and have dialed their
coaching into the power of love. Buddha talks about many
things, but love was always an essential element of the path to
full liberation, physically, mentally, and spiritually. One might
even say that the Buddha couldn't exist without love. And
without the Buddha, the powerful messages of this book and
my work could not have come to be.

Let's be clear about this: Buddha love is not the romantic
variety. It is different than our Western version and perhaps
more difficult to understand because of the cultural baggage we
carry from birth. For the Buddha, love is a deep understanding
of others coupled with a deep desire for their well-being.
With compassion, joy, kindness, and love, a leader is able
to help others develop their innate capacities to their full
human potential.

For the Buddha, love is a light in a tunnel that guides you
to your personal promised land. It extends respect to all even
in times of extreme challenge, giving unselfishly because others
are human beings like you and we are all a miracle waiting to
happen within a safe, caring environment, free of ridicule and
harsh criticism. Think about a tiny seed that has all it needs to
blossom into a beautiful flower when it is placed in rich soil
with clear sunlight and is watered every day. If you can imagine

The Competitive Buddha

each athlete, friend, or person in this way, your love could create a miracle every day. As Buddhist thought reminds us, "If we could see the miracle of a single flower, our whole life would change." The Buddha encourages all of us to radiate boundless love toward those in our lives.

While coaching others either in large groups or individually, I honestly do all I can to fight for and win the hearts of these great spirits. I believe love is the most powerful method to helping my athletes and seminarians achieve success. The element of love in coaching and leadership is so vital that I considered writing an entire book on this subject with the title, *For the Love of Coaching*. I believe that my success as a parent, coach, teacher, author, and human being will be measured by how much I've loved. If you aspire to be an extraordinary coach, you must have love in your coaching... No love, no coaching.

John Wooden, upon his retirement from basketball at UCLA, was asked by the media why he was so successful. His reply was: "It is simple; there was a lot of love in my coaching."

Grambling state football coach Eddie Robinson said after he replaced coach Bear Bryant atop football's wins list that the secret to his success was love. "Coaching is a profession of love. You can't coach athletes unless you love them." Loving athletes, in fact, will inspire and empower them to go the distance. Coach Dean Smith is an example of a loving coach. In his book *The Carolina Way*, he mentions, "I truly cared about what happened to our players at Carolina while in school and after they graduated. I became close to them." Love was what was central to the athlete-coach relationship at Carolina.

And then there is Stanford women's head basketball coach Tara VanDerveer. Having worked together for a while, it became obvious to me in the locker room, at practice, and during games that Tara genuinely loved her athletes. This enabled her to deeply connect with her team and adapt to the changing landscape of athletics. In a recent podcast I did with Tara, she mentioned how the power of love is crucial to getting the most from your athletes. At the end of the session, she gave me a homework assignment: She asked me to Google the meaning of her first name, Tara. I did and was shocked to find out that it means the "female Buddha." She is a Buddha servant leader with much love in her heart.

Perhaps underlying most difficulties athletes have with coaches is the deep longing we all have to be loved, cared for, respected, and cherished. According to the teachings of the Chinese sage Confucius, "When the ruler cherishes affection and love for his kindred, there will be no disaffection among members of his family." The best leaders really do care about those under their guidance. Military books are replete with stories of how the best of the officers loved and cared for those under their command. Sun-Tzu, in his book *The Art of War*, alludes to the importance of generals loving and taking care of the troops as one would take care of a child who was loved. By so doing, the chances for victory in all their endeavors were greatly enhanced.

Love has many far-reaching effects on the athletes under your Buddha leadership. For example, you don't win tough games with talent. You win tough games by being tough, and that toughness happens when there is love. When athletes feel safe, respected, and loved, they will relentlessly go the distance, giving it their all-out effort and dedication. Athletes will give up when tired, but with love, they are tenacious even if totally fatigued. With an environment of love modeled by the coach, athletes will always battle and fight to the death for something bigger than just winning—something greater than themselves. This was demonstrated in an extraordinary way when I was working with the athletes of the 2013 woman's lacrosse team at the University of North Carolina. They were exhausted in triple overtime yet never caved in because of the relentless love the staff and athletes had for each other. They fought for something greater than themselves as they won their first national championship.

In addition to this toughness factor, environments where love proliferates are filled with discipline. When athletes have love, they refuse to let their team and staff down, and this is what creates discipline in such caring and loving environments.

Now, how do you as a coach with heart demonstrate this intangible yet felt concept of love? I have many ideas that have stood the test of time.

To demonstrate a coach's traits of love and caring, I suggest that you try the "oneness rule": one athlete, one positive comment, and one day at a time. Of course, when you do this, it becomes contagious and just as with any often-repeated habit, you won't be able to stop, and you will see the results. You may say: "Hey, Britt, I love the way you show up ready to play each practice. You really set a terrific tone for this team." That will stay in her heart for at least three weeks, at which point it will be time to begin again.

Another way to demonstrate Buddha love is to send an email or text or leave a note in a locker telling another how in awe you are of him or her. Tell the group or team how fortunate you are to be a part of their amazing lives. But most of all, always, every day, hour, and minute, treat those you lead with respect and kindness and take good care of them. Be firm and set boundaries where and when needed, but always do it in the spirit of the warrior, just the same way that you love to be loved. When that happens, others will follow you to the ends of the earth.

Then there are those moments in life when you must critique an athlete on his or her performance. To do so in a loving, caring fashion, try the PCP method: *Positive* opening, direct *Critique*, *Positive* close. For example, you may say something like: "Hey, Chip, I love the way you come to practice ready to play. That shows good leadership on your part. Now, if you want to take it up a notch, try communicating more often while you're practicing to get your team to follow your directions. That's better leadership. Want you to know that you are an important part of our lacrosse family." How would you feel after such an interaction with your coach?

I want to remind you that the power of love to empower others to grow, expand, and develop personal potential must be taken seriously by all leaders if positive change is to take place. I believe that miracles happen when we use love as the bottom line in our environments and relationships. As a coach, love is my bottom line. I seek multiple ways to remove all barriers to love, such as fear, self-doubt, and uncertainty, and then watch the miracles unfold as a natural expression of that love.

When considering the importance of love in your coaching, you may want to remember this quote by iconic coach Phil Jackson:

"It takes a number of critical factors to win an NBA championship...
talent, creativity, intelligence, toughness, and luck. But if a team doesn't
have the most essential ingredient—love—none of those factors matter."
—Phil Jackson, Former NBA Head Coach
(Chicago Bulls and Los Angeles Lakers)

The Noble Eightfold Traits of Mindful Leaders

"He who walks the Noble Eightfold Path with unswerving determination is sure to reach Nirvana."

—Buddhist Thought

In this section of Part Three, I adapt the tenets of Buddhism's Noble Eightfold Path to define the primary behavioral traits and characteristics of the mindful Buddha leader. Yet there is something you must know before we proceed, and that is the importance of the original Four Noble Truths and their role in leading us to the Noble Eightfold Path.

In a nutshell, Buddha taught that life is suffering and that the primary cause of our suffering is our cravings, wants, and need for things to be different from the way they really are. When we wish to prolong pleasure or reduce pain, we suffer. For example, athletes suffer when they are injured, when they are losing, or when they are trying without success to extend a winning streak, make more money, or get more playing time. The good news is the Buddha has given us a pragmatic, useful way for silencing or eliminating our desires by giving us the fourth Noble Truth, which he called the Noble Eightfold Path.

These eight specific behaviors are not a dogma, and when practiced by leaders in all walks of life, they wake us up and set us free. They help us to realize that all things, both on and off the court, are in a constant state of flux. Until this thought is accepted as a basic truth, neither you nor I will be happy or be able to discover mastery in any aspect of life. And from my perspective, mastery is a blissful state of nirvana, as the Buddha mentions in the opening quote.

The steps along the path are: right viewpoint, right thinking, right speech, right action, right livelihood, right effort, right mindfulness, and right concentration.

I will address these sacred eight paths as they intimately relate to the behaviors and traits of the mindful Buddha leader. All of these items can help you to create good thoughts leading to masterful performance as a coach and Buddha athlete. What's important to understand is that each one of the eight traits and behaviors supports each of the others. Think of them not as a linear progression but rather as linked aspects: Like a circle, they are all interconnected and so are all interdependent on one another.

Right View

I address the Right View first because it is the forerunner of the entire Eightfold Path. It is where we begin, a guide for everything that follows. It is our foundation, helping us to stay on track and not get lost. It is like a GPS geotracker, or more like a road map, actually, to where we wish to go and how we wish to be. The Right View creates proper action, influencing the choices and decisions we make as leaders. If we have the right view, we can proceed without suffering according to the Buddha. The right view is that which conforms to the Four Noble Truths, and when we can see things from this balanced perspective, we become liberated from our suffering. Otherwise, we take a path which is contrary to the Noble Truths, and this creates suffering. Neither right nor wrong, this view is dynamic: One choice simply leads to the end of suffering; the other doesn't.

With all of this said, what is the Right View when it pertains to leadership and sports? From a Buddhist perspective, the Buddha coach and athlete is one who connects with and cares for all teammates. It means working together as all five fingers do on one hand: one heart, one soul, one purpose, one goal. When working with my teams, I often teach this step on the Eightfold Path by using the analogy of the five sticks. One stick alone is easily broken, but when bundled together, it's practically impossible to break them. Working together as a team and looking at the game as something much stronger and bigger than any one individual is what I consider the Right View. With individual sports like golf and tennis, the event is so much bigger than you, the individual.

The Right View is all about the right perspective when we coach and compete, a way of understanding that sees the game as a whole, one where you give your all for the higher purpose of everyone involved. It includes the view of your opponent as your partner, with each helping the other achieve higher performance; the view that loss is our greatest teacher' and the view that in sport, you are meant to have fun and feel joy. As a mindful coach, you can infuse the hearts of your athletes with these thoughts, expressing them as your personal view.

Right Thought

Right thinking is the result of the forerunner, Right View. The Right View facilitates your ability as coach and athlete to have the Right Thought. Such thinking directly impacts the rest of the Noble Eightfold Path.

Buddhist thought teaches that we are each shaped by our mind. We become what we think. We lead and perform as we think. We live as we think, and no one other than ourselves can alter our minds. We control our thoughts, and those thoughts control us. According to the Buddha, the mind is the ultimate cause of our suffering. It is also the source of our happiness. A tamed mind brings happiness; a wild mind brings unhappiness. In Buddhist thought, changing the suffering mind to the joyful mind is the key to a happy life.

When I am coaching athletes, I encourage them to be aware of how thoughts about missing a shot, dropping a pass, losing a race, or striking out feed the possibility of those results happening. I encourage them to consider how realistically, these things could happen, but that's okay and not the end of the world because there will be other chances. I ask them, as well as myself, to replace maladaptive thoughts with positive thinking, such as: I can do it, I'm strong, next time I'll get it done, I'm an awesome athlete, coach, leader.

There's a story that's been going around for half a century that is emblematic of the greatest battles we'll ever fight, the ones between our good and bad thoughts. An old and wise grandfather says to his grandson, "There is a fight inside me. It's between two wolves; one that is evil and filled with anger, hate, greed, envy, and resentment, and another wolf that is good and has joy, love, peace, hope, truth, compassion, and kindness." The grandson thought about it for a minute, then asked his grandpa, "Which one will win?" The elder's reply was simple: "The one who'll win is the one you feed."

Along the Noble Eightfold Path, a mindful coach knows that right thinking will cause freedom from suffering. We all suffer when we worry about outcomes and results. We also suffer when we try to hold on to victory and achievement. I call this negative uncontrollable process "stinking thinking." Buddhist thought teaches us to let go of our needs to not lose or to hold on to victory. These are uncontrollable. As a leader or coach, I ask others to care more about what you can control, such as your efforts, work ethic, and putting focus on all the little things, like diving for the 50/50 ball, playing tough defense, communicating on the field, encouraging teammates, and never giving up. This is the "Buddha Ball" that leads to Right Thought, which opens the door to mastery. It makes it easier to lead and compete with less fear, to be present in the moment, and to become more tolerant of the ebb and flow of your emotions, your game, your life. Such thought places you in the middle between loss and gain, pleasure and pain, fame and disgrace, praise and blame.

As a mindful coach, tell your athletes that their thoughts can strengthen or weaken them. They have an energy of their own. The direction your thoughts go is where you will go. And you can control your thoughts and mitigate your suffering on this planet, in your life, in your work, in your sport.

Going from Buddha to Bob Marley, in his "Redemption Song," Marley suggests that we must all work to emancipate ourselves from mental slavery. If we as leaders don't, who will? When we free ourselves from bad thoughts, we create greater peace, calm, confidence, and a stronger outlook in our team's sports culture. This inner battle can be won because each of us has the power of choice. Think about how you may be feeding the bad wolf thoughts and replace them with the more positive narrative. I suggest that you think about what makes you feel grateful in sports and life.

One of the strongest and most effective ways to take charge of your thoughts is with step three of the Noble Eightfold Path: Right Speech, which is coming up next.

Right Speech

According to the mindful leader, Right Speech involves five conditions: One must speak at the right time, speak only the truth, speak gently without hardness, speak words that benefit others, and speak with lovingkindness, avoiding all malice. The key factor in Right Speech is creating harmony and happiness among those you lead while at the same time avoiding harmful words in order to reduce suffering. All of this is relevant when speaking to oneself as well.

The basic rule of thumb for Right Speech is if it is helpful, true, factual, timely, and pleasing, then you may say it. If something is not pleasing, yet is helpful, true, and factual, you may need to choose the right time to say it. All Right Speech needs to be pleasing. All Right Speech gives rise to peace, happiness, and connection in oneself and others. If you as coach veer off this path, that's fine, but know that with such awareness, you can choose to get right back on track.

Sports leadership is a perfect venue for this in that it provides many opportunities to practice Right Speech. In the cultures I as coach help teams to develop, we choose to compete and live by values that enhance how we relate and speak to one another. Respect, compassion, joy, selflessness, love, trust, mindfulness, and positivity help to create environments where Right Speech can proliferate. There is no room for whining, drama, or harsh behavior in places that wish to inspire mastery.

Right Speech is rooted in the fundamental belief that we truly care for one another. Masterful performance and mindful leadership in sports is all about such caring. Steve Kerr, head coach of the champion Golden State Warriors, told me recently, "I want to make sure that my guys feel valued, respected, important, and relevant." When athletes feel this way, magic happens and they compete at higher levels. But how does he do this? How do any of us make this happen?

How can we best demonstrate our caring for each other? It's not about connecting my professional coaching head to your head. It's about connecting my human heart to your human heart, using Right Speech. The following can help you to better understand this factor in your coaching.

To connect my heart to yours, I imagine that I open the little door to my heart and become mindful of how I care for you. This "open door" policy reminds me to be caring, genuine, authentic, and vulnerable. I can then use Right Speech such as, "I love being with you. There's not another team (person) I'd rather be with than you right now."

How does that make you feel? How do you think your athletes would feel if they heard this? Have you ever said this to an athlete? Why not? If you do not do this, there's a chance you could lose them. But if you do it, you increase the chance of getting your team to go the distance, work harder, develop loyalty, and become mentally tougher. Performance on and off the court is all about how the coach leads with Right Speech; how you feel is how you'll perform. It's really quite simple: When you care for your athletes in this way, they reach their full potential. You can make a difference in how you impact others with regard to how they feel by utilizing what I call the RIVER effect.

Implementing kindness through Right Speech for all others is what the RIVER effect is truly about. The RIVER effect draws on a five-letter acronym that I use consistently as a reminder for me to be mindful and extend kindness in all my relationships. It helps me to connect and care more deeply. I do what I can to help others feel the RIVER and what it represents. In that regard, I want others to feel Relevant, Remarkable, Important, Inspired, Valued, Validated, Empowered, Excited, Respected, and Revered.

How do those you coach behave, act, play, work, and compete when they feel the river flowing through them? When you remember and adopt the RIVER acronym, you can easily create amazing opportunities to inspire, empower, validate, and show respect to others using Right Speech. It becomes a mindful touchstone that, when used, increases the chances that others will be loyal, go the distance, work harder, and develop mental strength.

The following are examples of Right Speech that you can use in coaching to share the RIVER effect with others.

- You're important to this team. We need your awesome efforts. (Relevant)

- I love your work ethic. It motivates all of us. (Remarkable)

- If you keep playing like that, you'll be one of the best athletes I've ever coached. (Inspired)

- We value your presence on this team. You bring out the best in everyone. (Valued)

- That last week of practice was one of your best so far. (Validated)

- I want to give you permission to keep being a great leader. (Inspired)

- When you play and compete like that, you're being a true champion. (Empowered)

- Without you, we wouldn't be the great team we are. (Revered)

- I appreciate and love how much you give of yourself to your teammates. (Important)

Golden State Warriors head coach Steve Kerr uses the RIVER concept on a consistent basis, and by so doing, gets the most from his players. Pete Carroll of the Seattle Seahawks is always looking for an opportunity to demonstrate similar caring strategies that help his athletes feel respected and important. I told him about the RIVER acronym, and he agreed how helpful that is in bringing out the best in others.

Cindy Timchal, winningest lacrosse coach ever, for both men and women, has adopted and adapted the RIVER effect to her coaching style. When she's mindful of using it, she notices that there is major player buy-in to her system. She bathes her athletes in the RIVER and then notices the tsunami—that is, how "the athletes are super willing to put it all out on the field."

While I didn't realize it at the time, my first and only meeting with Dean Smith, the iconic men's basketball coach at the University of North Carolina, showed me that he was brilliant at using the RIVER effect even though he hadn't consciously thought about it in this way. He was the kind of leader who used deep, genuine Right Speech. Following an intimate forty-five-minute meeting together, I felt so inspired, valued, and important that I committed myself to writing my book *Coaching with Heart*.

The RIVER effect fulfills all of the requirements of Right Speech: It is helpful, true, factual, and pleasing, and the time is always perfect for such words. Make the RIVER your go-to acronym for effective leadership.

Right Action

The fourth aspect of the Noble Eightfold Path is Right Action, and it relates to ethical conduct, right morality, and the ability to live harmoniously with others. According to Buddhist teacher Thich Nhat Hanh, Right Action happens when you do all things in mindfulness. When you do, you act in harmony with respecting life, you demonstrate generosity by giving to and serving others, you promote social justice, you avoid sexual misconduct and exploitation, and you pay attention to what you consume, choosing healthful foods and avoiding harmful intoxicants, and refrain from lying.

As it relates to sports, Right Action could influence your athletes' behavior, such as by decreasing showboating, trash-talking, or disrupting a practice or game. These common behaviors are a sign of disrespect for others. Buddhism teaches compassion and kindness, and these actions are the antithesis of such teaching. Phil Jackson has stated how engaging in the Right Action of compassion as a coach with his teams has proved to be one of the foundational building blocks of his championship teams.

Right Action is also about being honest. It applies to a coach's integrity and character. If you say you'll do something, you do it, even when no one is looking. Cheating is about doing all the illegal things that break the rules to gain advantage. Intentional fouls are harmful and disrespectful to an opponent. As a coach, be sure your athletes know this about their behavior.

Whining and creating unnecessary drama are both destructive actions. Also, selfishness gives rise to actions contrary to the Buddhist teaching of generosity. Right Action for both coaches and athletes is about giving and serving your team in a selfless way. When a coach asks an athlete to assume a certain role, it is accepted as a way to serve the team, a part of doing whatever it takes to make the team better. See the story about Andre Igoudala in the section on Selflessness in Part Two.

As coaches and athletes, we also want to pay strict attention to our diet. Many professional and collegiate programs that I serve have hired nutritional experts to help everyone make choices guided by right action with regard to health and wellness. Many of my teams have fruitful, helpful discussions that lead to big changes in alcohol consumption, especially during season. The deleterious effects of alcohol consumption on both leadership and performance are well documented.

Finally, we all are benefiting from social activism, such as the #MeToo movement as it relates to sexual misconduct by athletes. The Buddhist teaching of Right Action continues to help all of us address these current issues in sports. This is an issue relevant to all sports organizations.

Right Livelihood

The Buddha encourages us to engage in a meaningful livelihood involving compassionate activity and work. Understandably, we all have an economic aspect to our work and career. While we need to make a living, it is also possible to make a difference in the lives of others in the Buddhist sense. Work can be a calling to a spiritual practice, a place that deepens our awareness and humility. Whether you're a CEO of a corporation or the CEO of your family, a principal of a school or a janitor, an owner of a business or one of its employees, you can always choose to do your work with heart. How can your leadership work become meaningful?

The broad vision is to decide never to choose work that brings harm to others. You can't be kind in your personal life and cause harm professionally. This is a cause of cognitive dissonance and creates suffering, internal agitation, and remorse.

If you want a peaceful heart and a quiet soul, find a position of leadership that doesn't compromise your principles, one that is without serious contradictions of your ideals of love and compassion. If your intention is to help society in any way, perhaps you must follow a livelihood that promotes honesty, fairness, and good service to others.

How does this element of the Noble Eightfold Path relate to sport? It's short and simple...no need to get too complex. Sport is a business with many players. There's the management (especially in pro sports, like the general manager), there are the administrators (the athletic director), the coaches, the athletes, and the trainers. All these pieces of the whole pie fit into the definition of Right Livelihood explained above. If you follow the message of the Buddha, you will be on the way to Right Livelihood.

For example, I am hired by many organizations, programs, and teams as their sports psychologist and spiritual advisor. I *love* my work. It's not a job per se; it's a calling. Honestly, I don't work to make a living. I work to make a difference in the lives of all those who hire me. It is an honor to be asked to do this work. And interestingly enough, the more I focus on serving, giving, and making a difference, the greater living I make. It's all about creating meaning in this lifetime, and my mindful coaching work is a significant part of that.

This is a concept I teach to all the coaches with whom I work. In my book *Coaching with Heart*, I help leaders to align with a more mindful Eastern approach to their work by helping them understand the value of being in service to others and of finding ways to give love, time, and attention to their athletes.

This same concept holds true not just for coaches but for the athletes as well. Their work is to give selflessly to their team and to demonstrate connection and caring. The Buddhist Right Livelihood approach to leadership is fulfilled when we serve well in our work. This requires us to respect one another while keeping our ego in check. (See "Egolessness" in Part Two). Such a path will bring profound peace, joy, wisdom, and happiness in all the work you do, regardless of job title or status.

The Competitive Buddha

Right Effort

This section of the Noble Eightfold Path is also called Right Diligence, the development of positive heart-mind states through preventing the arising of doubt, worry, anger, stress, power, greed, fame, and insomnia leading to insufficient rest and sleep. The developing of good qualities is best facilitated with mindfulness, the subject of the next section.

Someone wise once said, "Live as if you'll die tomorrow." When you do, you live, coach, and lead with lovingkindness, harmony, and generosity, and focus only on that which is important. When Steve Jobs was diagnosed with cancer, he alluded to the notion that all expectations, fears, and loss fall away in the face of death, leaving only what is truly important. Remembering you are going to die is the best way to avoid thinking you have something to lose or something to gain. Buddhism supports this assessment in its teaching about impermanence. All things are fleeting, including winning and losing games in sport and life. With that I will segue into the meaning of Right Effort as it relates to sports.

To implement an awareness of the truth that these things are ephemeral, Right Effort is necessary. In athletics, I call it *Effort without Effort*. Care about your effort and work ethic, but not about outcomes and results. This makes it easier to compete because it frees you: There is less to worry about and less to fear because you can control the little things and not be concerned about the uncontrollable results. Clinging to the outcomes, titles, minutes played, or contracts negotiated is a futile effort that leads to suffering.

Try to stop caring about how you *do* and just think about how you can *be*. Be brave, courageous, patient, persistent, respectful, aware, positive, and kind. When I find that I am overly concerned with an outcome, I often tell myself, "To hell with it," and this helps me to be calmer and more relaxed. My advice is to follow the way of *Effort without Effort*.

You see it constantly in sports and exercise: When you decide to cut back, let up, and exert less effort, your performance begins to improve. This principle of effortless effort was successfully demonstrated years ago by Olympic runners Ray Norton, Tommie Smith, John Carlos, and Lee Evans. Their coach, Bud Winter, developed the 90 percent law. When runners try to perform at 100 percent, they get anxious and tense. Too much effort blocks their energy and life force and diminishes their power. Performing at nine-tenths effort is more relaxing and results in better outcomes—in this case, faster speed.

Let's say you're trying to run up a steep hill. The more effort you exert, the more difficult it seems to be. Rather than apply effort, enjoy the natural surroundings and try to glide rather than pushing yourself up. Rigidity sets in when anything reaches its full limit. When you do your weight training, for example, relax your muscles, yet keep your arms firm as you lift. Notice how much stronger you feel by not exerting as much. All of your physical activity will go up a notch as you begin to exert less. This is easily demonstrated by doing push-ups. Get in position, relax your arms and face, and effortlessly do five of them. Now, repeat the process using tensed arms. Notice how much easier it is when you apply less force, effort, and push. Maybe we should call them "rise-ups."

When you learn the advantage of paying attention to the energy flow and rhythms in your coaching and see how pushing or forcing is counterproductive, then you begin to apply this Buddha non-force way of effort to work and the rest of life. Oftentimes your inner turmoil, struggle, and pain related to your leadership are the result of your continual efforts to force what cannot be. You quickly enter a spiritual vacuum as frustration, anger, depression, and fear begin to take over as a result of your futile attempts to control the uncontrollable.

When you find yourself forcing and exerting to finish a project, you increase the chance of getting stuck. Authors are famous for hitting "writer's block" when they try too hard to be creative. When blockage happens, focus on the inner spiritual elements of joy, beauty, and the flow of your art. Notice how much better you feel about your work as it begins to go more smoothly. Tell yourself that you're simply here to enjoy the task, and don't perseverate on the outcome. Ask yourself, "How can I do it more effortlessly?" Then follow your own advice. You practically have to "not care" yet not be totally "care-less" in this delicate balance of effort without effort.

Notice the peace you experience in coaching when you choose to step aside as tension mounts, rather than forcing your opinion on others; when you choose to enter a relationship and you don't force the process; and when you choose not to push for an unnaturally speedy recovery when sick or injured. Martial artists have understood for centuries that the less effort you exert, the more proficient and spiritually sane you will become in all that you do.

When we master this concept, which we can accomplish by simply coming back to it when off track, we begin to function more in harmony with the Buddhist Middle Way, paradoxically employing effort, yet without effort.

Right Mindfulness

According to Zen teacher Thich Nhat Hanh, Right Mindfulness is the foundation of ancient Buddhist teaching. When Right

Mindfulness is present, the Four Noble Truths and the Noble Eightfold Path are present as well. The most well-recognized Western definition of mindfulness comes from one of the most prominent, best-known teachers of the concept—Jon Kabat-Zinn. According to him, mindfulness is "paying attention in a particular way, on purpose, in the present moment."

Mindfulness, in Buddhist terms, is being aware and awake to the present moment on a consistent basis. This awareness helps you to see clearly and act more appropriately with your actions, words, and decisions in all aspects of life. In his classic book *Be Here Now*, the late Ram Dass teaches us how wakefulness is about being alert to the present without letting past experiences or fears of the future color and obscure this moment.

James Baraz, says in his book *Awakening Joy*, "Mindfulness is simply being aware of what is happening right now without wishing it were different; enjoying the pleasant without holding on when it changes; being with the unpleasant without fearing it will always be this way."

In Buddhism, we are introduced to the notion of the "Monkey Mind." It is a mind that is out of control, agitated, and scattered. Buddhist mindfulness practices are designed to help leaders quiet these monkeys, tame them, and bring the mind back to the here and now. One of these practices is called meditation, a skill I will address and teach in the very next section.

Why is it important to develop a state of Right Mindfulness? In my teaching and work with athletes, coaches, teams, and others, I encourage them to practice mindfulness because it helps you to be happy and improves the quality of how you live, what you do, and how you do it. It feels good to be relaxed, calm, and peaceful. It lowers stress, anxiety, worry, and depression, all important variables that must be contained if we want to experience masterful performance. It helps you gain perspective on the up and down, gain and loss nature of life… and, of course, athletics.

Speaking of sports, what athlete or coach doesn't experience the Monkey Mind by bouncing back and forth between our past mistakes, future outcomes, and potential injury? As a result, we can get distracted from what's happening right here, right now.

To help his team develop a strong sense of such mindfulness, coach Phil Jackson of the LA Lakers created the "warrior room" at their practice facility in El Segundo, California. In that sacred space, with the help of author George Mumford, team members would come in to practice mindful meditation. It was voluntary, but athletes like Kobe Bryant used this time effectively. When Michael Jordan was with the Chicago Bulls, he embraced the value of mindfulness and soon proclaimed, "This Buddhist stuff really works."

I know that sports are one of the best venues to practice mindfulness. You need not be a Buddhist monk to have a successful practice. I have experienced the growth of mindfulness over a forty-year span in my career to a point where today, it is profoundly mainstream. My teams at all levels of performance don't just want it, they crave it. Many top athletes and coaches in sports embrace the concept of mindfulness as a way to quiet their minds and move to a place of deeper involvement in their sport for its own sake. Mindfulness is the most essential key to manifesting the competitive Buddha, effective leadership, and masterful performance as you begin to consistently tap into the flow of each event in the present moment.

As I mentioned earlier, the next section of Part Three will be devoted to this topic and will guide you through the process of mindful meditation, the same one I've used with 115 championship teams over the past thirty years.

Right Concentration

It appears that Right Concentration from a Buddhist perspective means keeping one's attention steadily on one single aspect of your environment, such as a word, an object, your breath, or the color blue in the fire burning in a fireplace, and continuing to do that for extended periods of time. Such concentration is the special ingredient of Buddhist Vipassana meditation practice.

Concentration requires us to slow down of our mental activity. When we are multitasking or thinking of several things at once, our minds are in a beta brain wave state of between seventeen and twenty cycles per second. With meditation, those brain waves can slow down to seven to ten cycles per second, a rhythm called the 'alpha' state. Such states of alpha can be achieved in a quiet place using Buddhist meditation techniques. This is basically a simple breathing process that requires practice before the mind can achieve quiet. I will help you with this in the next section by getting you to fix your mind on the breath to the exclusion of all else and to get back to that breath when you wander, which you will.

The ability to stay on task without distraction or the mind wandering is extremely beneficial in leadership, coaching, and masterful sports performance. I can attest to this, having taught meditation to thousands of athletes and coaches throughout my career. Recently, mindful awareness has become an essential ingredient in the world of athletics.

The Competitive Buddha

Imagine that no time is left on the clock, your team is down by one point in a vital basketball game, and you're shooting the front end of a one and one. The pressure is enormous, and the distraction is unreal. How do you concentrate when all around you is chaotic, with so much riding on your mind's ability to focus? Tiger Woods always had the ability to focus like a laser beam since he was a child (see "The Way of the Tiger" in Part One). He has been quoted as saying, "A bomb could go off, and I wouldn't even know. That's the focus I had." This is a skill that can be learned.

Leading with the Strength of Ten Tigers

"If you know the art of breathing, you have the
strength, wisdom, and courage of ten tigers. The
quiet, focused mind can pierce through stone."
—Mindfulness proverb

"If your mind is empty, it is always ready for anything; it
is open to everything. In the beginner's mind, there are
many possibilities; in the expert's mind, there are few."
—Shunryu Suzuki, Zen Buddhist Monk

The practice of meditation, often referred to as "the still point," is a learned skill that when developed, can impact not just your leadership and coaching, but your entire life. It is important to know that the Buddha believed that effective mindful leadership is developed with an open heart through the practice of meditation.

Over the years, meditation has become a household word—a universal concept that when applied to sports can help you to experience a feeling of mastery and perform at your very best. Motivation, competition, training, injury recovery, and focus are a few of the ways I apply meditation in working with athletics. It is how we tame what the Buddha refers to as the "monkey mind."

Phil Jackson has shown his mastery of using mindful meditation with his Bulls and Lakers teams, on his way to winning a total of eleven championship rings. In Phil's book by the same name, *Eleven Rings: The Soul of Success*, he devotes several detailed pages to his thoughts about, and personal practice of the meditation approach he used for his team, an approach detailed in Shunryu Suzuki's renowned book *Zen Mind, Beginner's Mind.*

To help his players on both teams to quiet the chatter of their minds and focus on the competitive nature of the game, he introduced them to the concept of mindfulness meditation, based on a practice he had learned years before. He would get the players to sit in a room for ten or so minutes together. As I previously mentioned, he called it "the warrior room." He wasn't trying to make them Buddhist monks; it was to bring them close and bond them at the heart.

All of the athletes who took part in this voluntary exercise loved it. It was a special, unified group, one that was, in the words of Vietnamese Buddhist monk Thich Nhat Hanh, "dwelling happily in the present moment" with quiet, simple, and clear minds. Jackson found through such practice that when athletes immerse themselves fully in the moment, they develop a deeper, stronger, mindful awareness of what's happening right now in the present moment. And in Jackson's words, this "leads to a greater sense of oneness, the essence of teamwork."

As a way to help his athletes foster team connection, cohesion, and a sense of unity, Phil Jackson applauds the value of mindfulness meditation in increasing the team's ability to break out of their me-oriented attitudes and giving them the opportunity to consider shifting to more of a focus on "we."

In his brilliant book on this process, Jackson quotes the thirteenth century Buddhist priest and teacher Nichiren:

> *The spirit of many in body, but one in mind, prevails among the people, [so] they will achieve all their goals; whereas if one in body, but different in mind, they achieve nothing remarkable.*

The following is an inspirational story about mindfulness meditation. During the Chinese cultural revolution of the 1960s, Chinese pianist and composer Liu Shih-Kun was incarcerated for six years with no piano and no paper to write on. During his incarceration, he practiced his music in his head, mindfully visualizing himself playing at a high level over and over. He even composed a concerto memorized it, and retained his recollection of how to play it. In 1973, following his release from prison, Liu played before his peers and was deemed to be even better than before he was locked up. This is what the power of mindfulness meditation can accomplish.

And it is apparent in all sentient beings. You may have noticed that animals instinctively employ a method of stillness in nature; they all meditate. Observe the heron poised motionless on one leg, the monkey climbing to the uppermost branch, the snake basking in the warmth of the summer sun, or the cat lying on a pillow, its eyes focused on a small object. Speaking of cats, I observed my cat, Simon, sitting and staring at the fireplace watching the flames dance for twenty minutes without movement. He was in the zone.

The version of meditation that I teach is a simple variation on a 2,500-year-old Buddhist form of meditation called *Vipassana* meditation, a Pali word meaning *insight*. It relies on your ability to focus on your natural breathing patterns as you sit quietly in the absence of distraction. This helps to clear the mind and create an in-the-moment experience. Sophisticated in its simplicity, this meditation does require consistency of practice, like any skill. It will help you to focus your attention and awareness in the moment and become more mindful in the here and now.

To begin, get comfortable sitting in a chair or on the floor—wherever you can be free of distraction or noise. Close

The Competitive Buddha

your eyes to better concentrate and focus on the natural movement of your breath. See and feel your breath. On the in breath, imagine your hand pulling your breath up from the heart, up through your neck, to the crown of your head. Then feel the out breath, and imagine gently pushing the breath back down with your hand to your heart. Repeat this process for several breaths. If your mind wanders, that is natural. Just quietly say inside, "Wandering, come back," and then immediately focus again on the pattern of your breathing. You can do this for three, five, ten, or more minutes—for as long as you like. This creates a still point inside, a place of inner calm, clarity, peace, and quiet, which becomes the basis for feeling mindful.

One variation I suggest is that after watching your breath for as many minutes as you'd like, you can switch to visualizing your intended performance outcome and how to move to be most effective. When you are able to maintain this state of mind for several minutes, you can choose to visualize yourself coaching; feel what it's like to be the Buddha mindful leader using all the traits discussed in this part of the book on mindful leadership. Actually see your athletes, hear your own voice, and feel your presence as envision yourself leading, guiding, and coaching them to inner places where they follow your directives and go the distance for you. The operative word here is the word "*feel*." Feeling yourself being this effective, mindful coach infuses your nervous system with this Buddha way, resulting in the your being able to carry out these mindful behaviors when called upon in real life.

When you strengthen the mind through meditation in this way, your actions and behaviors in everyday life gradually shift and impact the way you perform. This method also enables you to take a good look at yourself and make the appropriate changes in how you accomplish your dreams.

Of course, meditation practice is like physical training; it is exercise for the mind. Such exercise helps you to develop greater mental and emotional strength. Well-conducted scientific studies have demonstrated that after only eight weeks of meditation practice, participants can experience much lower levels of anxiety, higher levels of performance, a significant rise in positive emotions, and more happiness.

Part Four

THE SOUND OF ONE HAND CLAPPING

Mindful Zen Stories to Elevate Your Game

One of my absolute favorite activities to do with my athletic teams to provide insight, perspective, and inspiration about sports and life is to tell compellingly profound Zen Buddhist stories, both ancient and modern, with lessons that often shape how those who listen compete, play, and live.

The great teachers of all time have used parables and stories to convey valuable lessons. My purpose is to pass on ideas and wisdom taught by the Buddha to my athletes. Hopefully from my doing this, they will remember these wonderful tales for many years to come. Buddhism comes from the word *budhi*, meaning 'to awaken.' You can awaken in many different ways, and one of the best is through stories and parables. Stories provide so much; they tug at your emotions, and you tend to connect with them on a personal level. Stories point the way.

These powerful teaching tales, which I incorporate into my work, inspire us all on our journey to use competitive Buddha wisdom to raise the level of our game. They don't just inform, they entertain. The lessons learned are the fundamental building blocks and essential concepts of the Buddha way. My wish is that by telling these tales, you will strengthen your resolve to be free, gain peace, and perform at higher levels on this masterful journey. With experiential insight derived from these narratives, you will renew your commitment to being a better version of yourself in sport and life.

There is no need to become a Zen master practicing zazen sitting on some mountaintop. Just be you and observe the relevancy of each story to your specific activity and life. These compelling and deep Zen perspectives can give you a refreshingly expanded outlook and insight into the spiritual side of sports. Think of these stories as catalysts and guides that will help you apply the Buddha way to sports, as well as helping you to apply insights from sports to the vicissitudes of life. These tales will encourage, empower, and inspire you to develop a more thorough understanding of yourself, sports, and life on the way to becoming a wiser human being.

These parables and stories were translated into English from a book called *Shaseki-shu*, written late in the thirteenth century by the Japanese Zen teacher Maju Ichien. Later on, these stories were gathered and compiled by Nyogen Senzaki, a Zen monk, in his book *101 Zen Stories*. He worked together with poet and author Paul Reps to compile all these stories into a modern volume called *Zen Flesh, Zen Bones.* These books are the inspiration and guides from which I chose and wrote my interpretations of the following thirty-two stories.

The Sound of One
Hand Clapping

The master of a Japanese temple had a young student who was only twelve years old. His pupil would watch the older disciples visit the master's room each morning and evening to receive instruction in sanzen [Zen teachings], in which they were given individual koans to stop mind-wandering. The youngster wished to do sanzen also.

"Wait a while," said the master. "You are too young."

But the child insisted, so the teacher finally gave his permission.

In the evening, the little boy went at the proper hour to the threshold of the sanzen room, striking the gong to announce his presence and bowing thrice respectfully outside the door before going to sit before the master in respectful silence.

"You can hear the sound of two hands when they clap together," said the master. "Now show me the sound of one hand."

The boy bowed and went to his room to consider the problem. From his window, he could hear music being played by the geishas. "Ah, I have it!" he declared.

The next evening, when his teacher asked him to demonstrate the sound of one hand, the lad began to play the music of the geishas.

"No, no, no," said his master, "That will never do. That is not the sound of one hand. You haven't got it at all."

Thinking that the sound of the music might get in the way of a solution, the boy moved his lodgings to a quieter place, then he meditated once more. "What can the sound of one hand be?" He happened to hear the sound of some water dripping. "I have it!" he exclaimed.

When he next came into his teacher's presence, the boy imitated the sound of dripping water.

"What is that?" asked the master. "That is the sound of dripping water, but it is not the sound of one hand. Try again."

The youngster tried in vain to hear the sound of one hand clapping during his meditations. He heard the sighing of the wind. But that was not the right sound.

He heard the an owl's cry. This was not the right sound either.

The sound of one hand clapping was not the buzz of the locusts.

The boy visited the master with different sounds more than ten times in all, but none of them were right. For nearly a year, the lad wondered what the sound of one hand's clap might be.

At last, he entered the state of true meditation and transcended all sounds. "I could collect no more sounds," he explained afterwards, "so I reached the soundless sound."

He had finally realized the sound of one hand.

The lesson here is the value of deep meditation and how it helps blank out sound as you sit in silence. No need to search for something that doesn't exist. One hand clapping is silence. Why and how is this relevant to you in sports and life? What do you think is the lesson from this story?

Empty Your Cup

A venerable Japanese master during the late 1800s received a visiting university professor who came to ask him about Zen.

The master served the professor tea, pouring until his visitor's cup was full—but then he kept on pouring. The professor watched the cup overflowing until he could restrain himself no longer and blurted out, "It is completely full. No more will go into the cup!"

The master replied, "Like this cup, you are full of your own opinions and speculations. How can I show you Zen unless you first empty your cup?"

The lesson from this story is about the importance of being open-minded. How and why is this relevant to sports and your life? Perhaps you have a different interpretation of this story. Why and how is that relevant to you?

Life Is Very Brief

The emperor's teacher used to travel alone, and despite his highly placed position, would often dress as an impOverished wanderer. Once while on a journey to the capital city, he came to a tiny village. A heavy rain was falling that evening, and he was thoroughly wet; his straw sandals had fallen apart on the muddy roads. Near the village, he noticed several pairs of sandals in the window of a farmhouse and decided to buy some new ones, hoping for more comfort as they would be dry.

Seeing how wet he was, the woman who offered him the sandals invited him to stay in her home for the night. With thanks, the teacher accepted. He entered the house and recited a sutra before the family shrine. Then the woman introduced him to her mother and her children. Noticing that the entire family seemed full of sorrow, he asked what was wrong.

"My husband is a gambler as well as a drunkard," the woman told him. "When he chances to win, he drinks and becomes abusive. When he loses, he borrows money from everyone he knows who will lend him anything more. Sometimes when he gets completely sloshed, he doesn't come home at all. What can I do?"

"I will help him," the teacher said. "Here, take this money. Get me a gallon of fine wine and something delicious to eat, then you go to bed and try to get some sleep. I will sit in contemplation before the shrine."

When the man of the house returned around midnight, three sheets to the wind, he bellowed, "Hey, wife! I'm home! What have you got for me to eat?"

"I have something for you," said the teacher. "I ended up getting caught in the rain, and your wife kindly invited me to stay for the night. In return for her magnanimity, I bought a bottle of wine and some fish, so you may as well have them."

The drunk was delighted; he immediately drank the wine and then laid himself down on the floor. Meanwhile, the teacher sat in meditation beside him.

In the morning, when the husband awoke, he had no memory of the previous night. "Who are you? Whence come you?" he inquired of the teacher, who was still meditating.

"I am the emperor's teacher, and I am going on to the capital city," replied the Zen master.

Hearing that the unexpected guest in his home was the teacher of his emperor, the hungover man was terribly ashamed and apologized profusely.

The teacher smiled and told him, "Everything in this life is impermanent. Life is very brief. If you continue to gamble and drink, you will run out of time to accomplish anything else, and besides that, you will cause your family further suffering as well."

One of the lessons from this story is about making good use of your time and being the best version of yourself possible. Why and how is this relevant to you in sports and your life? And what other interpretation might you have; why and how is what you see in the story relevant?

 The Competitive Buddha

Is That So?

A wise Zen master was esteemed by his neighbors as they saw he lived a pure life.

A Japanese couple who owned a food store near him had a beautiful young daughter. Without any knowledge of her having spent any time with boys, her parents were shocked to discover that their daughter was with child.

Her parents were very angry and pressed her to name the baby's father. She would not say who it was that had made her pregnant, but after much badgering, she at last told them it was the Zen master.

In great anger, the parents went to speak with him. "Is that so?" were the only words he would say in answer.

After the child was born, the girl's parents brought the baby to the master. By this point, he had lost his good reputation, which did not bother him, but he cared for the child with kindness and dedication. He bought milk and everything else the little one needed from his neighbors.

A year later, the young mother couldn't stand it any longer; she told her parents who the father really was: a young man who was a worker in the village fish market.

The girl's parents at once went to the Zen master to ask his forgiveness and get the child back again, all the while apologizing profusely.

In his unperturbed wisdom, the master was willing. Returning the child to the family, the only words he said were, "Is that so?"

The lessons here are how best to react when accused falsely of doing something wrong, and how to do the right thing. Why and how are these lessons relevant to you in sports and life? And you may see the story in a different light. How and why is that way of seeing it relevant to you?

Stand Up and Be Counted

Two dozen monks and one nun were meditating with a certain Zen master.

The nun was very pretty even though her head was shaved bare and her dress was plain. Quite a number of the monks had secretly fallen in love with her. One of them a love letter to her demanding a private meeting.

But the nun did not reply. The next day, however, after the master gave a lecture to the group, she arose, and addressing the monk who had written her the insistent letter, said, "If you really love me that much, come embrace me now."

The lesson from this story is to be true to your word, live with integrity, and stand up and be counted when it matters, regardless of consequences. Why and how is this relevant to you in sports and life? What could be another way of looking at this story?

Feeling Powerful Waves

Many, many years ago, there lived a famed wrestler who was immensely strong and well-versed in the art of wrestling. When he wrestled in private, he won even when wrestling his teacher, but in public bouts, he was so painfully shy that his own students threw him.

The wrestler felt he should visit a Zen master and ask for help. A wandering Zen teacher was at a little temple nearby for a short time, so the wrestler went to see him and told him of his situation.

The teacher advised the wrestler to remain in the temple overnight, telling him this: "Imagine that you are no longer a wrestler who is afraid, but rather powerful, billowing waves of the sea. You are huge waves that are able to sweep everything before them and swallow all in their path. Hold this vision in your mind, and you will be the greatest wrestler in any land."

The teacher went to bed; meanwhile, the wrestler sat in meditation trying to inwardly envision himself as great waves. Many different things went through his mind; but eventually, he turned more and more to the feeling of being the waves. As the hour became later and later, the waves grew larger and larger. The waves swept away the flowers in their vases; even the statue of the Buddha in the shrine was flooded with their force. Before sunrise, the temple was nothing but the ebb and flow of an enormous sea.

When morning came, the teacher found the wrestler meditating with a faint smile on his face. "Now, nothing can disturb you," said the master, patting the wrestler's shoulder. "You have become those waves. You will sweep everything before you."

That same day, the wrestler entered the wrestling contests, winning every one. After that, no one was able to defeat him.

The lesson here is about the power of the mind and how visualizing something as if it is so helps it grow. Why and how is this relevant to you in sports and life?

Do you have a more relevant interpretation that fits your life especially well?

What might that be?

The Competitive Buddha

Making a Gift of the Moon

Once there was a Zen master who lived the simplest possible sort of life in a tiny hut at the foot of a mountain. One evening, a robber broke into the hut, only to find that there was nothing inside to steal.

The master, returning, caught him. "You may have come a great distance to visit me," he told the thief, "and you should not leave empty-handed. Please take my clothes as a gift."

The thief was bewildered by this turn of events. He took the clothes and slunk away.

The Zen master sat naked at his window; watching the moon, he mused, "Poor fellow; I wish I could give him this beautiful moon."

The lesson here is about giving to those in need and the reward of doing so. Why and how is this relevant to your sports and life?

Perhaps you see another valid message. Why and how is it relevant to you?

Is That Burden Still Weighing You Down?

Two Zen monks were traveling together down a muddy road as a heavy rain fell. Coming around a bend, they met a comely girl dressed in a silk kimono and sash who was unable to cross the muck of the intersection without ruining her costly clothes.

At once, the first monk beckoned to her, saying, "Come on, girl." Lifting her slender weight in his arms, he carried her safely across the muddy road.

The second monk was silent until that evening, when they reached a temple inn and obtained lodgings for the night. But then he no longer could restrain himself. "We monks never go near females," he told the first monk, "especially young and beautiful girls, as it is dangerous. Whyever did you do that?"

"I left the girl there," said the first monk. "Are you still carrying her?"

The lesson here is about letting go of the emotional weight of guilt and moving on, especially if your intention is pure. Why and how is this relevant to you and your sports and life?

And how else could we interpret this passage?

Not Far from Buddhahood

A university student who was visiting a close friend asked him, "Have you ever read the Christian Bible?"

"No, read it to me," his friend replied.

The student, opening the Bible, read from the Gospel of St. Matthew: "And why take ye thought for raiment? Consider the lilies of the field, how they grow. They toil not, neither do they spin, and yet I say unto you that even Solomon in all his glory was not arrayed like one of these... Take therefore no thought for the morrow, for the morrow shall take thought for the things of itself."

His dear friend declared, "Whoever uttered those words is someone I consider to be an enlightened man."

The student went on reading: "Ask and it shall be given you, seek and ye shall find, knock and it shall be opened unto you. For everyone that asketh receiveth, and he that seeketh findeth, and to him that knocketh, it shall be opened."

His friend remarked in response, "That is exceptional. Whoever said that is not far from Buddhahood."

What is the relevancy of these words for you in sports and in life? How can you implement them to your advantage?

And what could be yet another way of looking at this passage?

In the Moment

A man crossing an open field encountered a tiger. He fled, with the tiger after him. As the man came to the edge of a cliff, he took hold of the root of a wild vine and swung himself out over the edge, with the tiger sniffing at him from above. Trembling, the man looked over to the ground below, where another tiger was waiting to eat him. Only the vine supported the man in this moment of mortal danger.

Then two mice, a white mouse and a black mouse, started to gnaw at the vine, eating it away little by little. At that moment, the man saw a deliciously ripe strawberry hanging near him. Clinging to the vine with one hand, he picked the strawberry with the other. How sweet it tasted!

The lesson here is that regardless of the past and the dangers that may loom in the future, it is important to stay present and live in the moment, appreciating what is sweet in the present. Why and how is this relevant to you in sports and life?

My Heart Burns Like Fire

Upon arriving, the first Zen teacher ever to come to America says,
"My heart burns like fire, but my eyes are as cold as dead ashes."
He set forth the following rules, which he himself followed every day
of his life:

In the morning before even putting on clothing, light incense
and meditate.

Go to bed at a regular hour. Take in food at regular intervals,
eating with moderation and never to the point of feeling full.

Receive a guest with the same frame of mind you have when
you are by yourself. When alone, maintain the same mindset you
have when you receive guests.

Watch what you say, and whatever you say, act in
accord with it.

When an opportunity shows up, do not let it go by, yet always
think twice before acting.

Do not regret the past. Look to the future.

Have the fearless demeanor of a hero and the loving heart
of a child.

Each night when you go to bed, sleep as if you had started your
last sleep. When you awaken, leave your bed behind instantly as if
you had thrown away an old pair of shoes.

What do you believe the message or lesson from this story to
be? Why and how does it relate to sports and life?

What is your take on this, and why and how is that relevant
to you now?

Three Days Longer

One summer, a student from a southern island of Japan came to visit a Zen teacher of note during a time of retreat and study.

The teacher gave the student a problem to solve: "Hear the sound of one hand."

Although the student attempted to break through to the answer for three years, he could not pass the test. One night, he came to the teacher in tears. "I must return south ashamed and embarrassed," the pupil said, "for I cannot solve this problem."

"Wait one week longer, meditating constantly," advised the wise man. But still no enlightenment came to the student. "Keep trying for another week," the teacher told him. The student obeyed, but to no avail.

"Yet another week." Still further meditation on the question was in vain. In desperation, the student begged to be released, but the teacher asked for one more meditation of five days' length. But these days, too, were without success. Then the wise man said, "Meditate for three days longer, then if you fail to arrive at enlightenment, you had better kill yourself."

On the second day after that, the student was enlightened.

The lesson here could possibly be the value of adversity and urgency to motivate behavior. Why and how is this relevant to you in sports and life, particularly if or when life (career, position, work) is on the line?

Trading Dialogue for Lodging

Any wandering monk can stay overnight in a Zen temple so long as he can make and win an argument about Buddhism with the monks who live there; but if he is defeated, he has to move on and find somewhere else to stay.

Two brother monks lived together at a temple in northern Japan. The older one had much learning, but the younger one was not only stupid but had only one eye.

A wandering monk came to the temple asking for lodging by challenging them to a proper debate about the essential teachings. The older brother, who was tired that day from a great deal of study, told the younger monk to take his place, cautioning him, "Go and ask that the dialogue be conducted in silence."

So the young monk and the stranger monk went to the shrine and sat down.

Shortly afterwards, the visiting monk arose; he went to the older brother, saying, "Your young brother monk is an excellent fellow. He defeated me."

"Relate how the dialogue went to me," said the older monk.

"Well," the traveler explained, "first I held up one finger, representing the Buddha, the enlightened one. So he held up two fingers, symbolizing the Buddha and his teaching. I help up three fingers, signifying the Buddha, his teaching, and his disciples, all living a life dedicated to harmony. Then he clenched his fist and shook it in my face, to represent that all three of these come to be from one realization. In this way, he won, so I have no right to stay here for the night since he gained the victory." With this declaration, the traveling monk departed.

"Where is that visiting fellow?" the younger one asked, running in to bespeak his elder brother.

"I hear that you won the debate."

"Won it? Forget winning, I'm going to beat him up."

"Describe the course of the debate," asked the older monk.

"Why, the moment he saw me, he held up one finger, offering me insult by pointing out that I have only one eye. Since he was a visiting stranger, I thought I ought to show him courtesy, so I held up two fingers, offering congratulations that he has two eyes. Then the rude scoundrel held up three fingers, signifying that between the two of us, we only have three eyes total. This made me very angry, so I started to punch him, but he ran out of the room, and that ended it!"

> The lesson here may be that sometimes our perceptions of things are just stories we make up when indeed the truth is quite different. Why and how is this relevant to you in sports and life? Do you have a different interpretation that makes sense to you?

The Treasure Is Already Inside

A traveler came to visit a Zen master in China. The master asked:
"What do you seek?"

"Enlightenment," replied the traveler.

"You have your own treasure house. Why do you seek a treasure
house outside?" replied the teacher.

"But where is my treasure house?" wondered the traveler
in confusion.

The master answered: "What you are asking is your
treasure house."

At that moment, the visitor was enlightened! From that day
forward, he exhorted his friends "Open your own treasure house
and use the treasures you find within."

One interpretation of this lesson is that oftentimes we seek the
good outside when indeed we already have it within us but fail
to notice its presence. Why and how is this relevant to you in
sports and life?

Perhaps another interpretation of this lesson works better for
you. What might that be?

The Authentic Self

Long ago, a noted Zen teacher was the head of a great cathedral in the city of Kyoto. One day, the governor of Kyoto came to call on the Zen master for the first time.

The governor's attendant presented his card, which bore the words 'Kitagaki, Governor of Kyoto.' "I have no business with such a person," the Zen master told the governor's man. "Tell him to get out of here."

The man returned with the card and apologies. "That was my mistake," the governor said; and taking a pencil, he scratched out the words 'Governor of Kyoto.' "Go and ask the master again."

"Oh, is that Kitagaki?" the teacher asked when he saw the card. "I want to see him!"

The lesson for me in this passage is that of humility, egolessness, and authenticity. If so, why and how is this relevant to you in sports and life?

Also, what could possibly be an interpretation that makes more relevant sense to you?

The Unseen Sutras of Compassion

A dedicated Zen devotee in Japan made a decision that he would publish the sutras, which were then available only in Chinese. Wood blocks would be carved to print the books in an edition of seven thousand copies, an enormous undertaking.

To raise funds for this imposing project, he began traveling to collect donations to pay for the printing blocks to be made. Occasionally, a few well-to-do donors would contribute as much as a hundred pieces of gold to the purpose, but most of the time, the donations he received were only a few small coins. He thanked each donor with an equally appreciative demeanor. After ten years of this fundraising journey, at last the devotee had collected enough money to begin the task.

At that time, the largest river in the region overflowed, causing flooding, famine, and a great deal of suffering, so he took the funds he had collected to print the books and spent the money to feed people who had nothing, saving them from starvation. Then the devotee began his fundraising work anew.

After several more years spent in raising funds, a terrible epidemic spread throughout the country. Again the devotee gave away the money he had collected to alleviate the suffering of his people.

Once more he started collecting funds for the publication of the sutras; and after twenty more years, his wish was fulfilled. The wood blocks used to print the first edition of the sutras in Japanese can be seen today in an ancient Japanese monastery.

The people of Japan tell the story that this Zen devotee had three sets of sutras made, and that the first two invisible sets were even greater than the last.

The lesson here points to the power of compassion and selflessness when giving to those in need. Those who are last will be first. Why and how is this relevant to you in sports and life?

Perhaps you have an additional interpretation that makes sense to you as well. What might that be?

The Competitive Buddha

Zen Mind

A disciple started dedicated study of Zen at the age of sixty, continuing until he was eighty years old, at which age he attained enlightenment.

He then became a teacher of Zen from the age of eighty to one hundred and twenty years old.

One day, a student asked, "If I haven't got anything in my mind, what should I do?"

"Throw it out," the old teacher told him.

"But if I haven't anything in mind, how can I throw it out?" the student demanded.

"Well," said the master, "if you can't throw it out, then carry it out."

The lesson here is that even if you are thinking your mind is empty, it is filled with that particular thought. For me, to quiet the mind and discover calm, I must meditate daily. Why and how is this relevant to you in sports and life?

Also, what other take on this story might you have, and why is that concept relevant?

The Thief Whose Path
Was Changed

One night when a Zen master was reciting sutras as usual, a thief came in menacing him with a sharp sword, demanding his money or his life.

The teacher told him, "Do not disturb me. Go and find the money for yourself, it is in that drawer." Then he began his recitation anew.

After a little while, he stopped and called out, "Don't take it all. I need some to pay my taxes, as they are due tomorrow."

The marauder started to make his way out, having gathered up most of the money. "Thank a person when you are given a gift," the master added. The man gave the teacher his thanks and then took off.

A few days later, the fellow was arrested; when interrogated, he confessed among other crimes to the offense against the wise teacher. But when the teacher was called as a witness against the man, he declared, "This man is no thief, at least not as far as I am concerned. I gave him that money, and he thanked me for it."

After he had completed the duration of his prison sentence for his various crimes, the man returned to the Zen master and became his disciple.

The lesson here could have something to do with acceptance and detachment and not trying to force your will on another. Why and how is this relevant to you and your sports and life?

It may very well be that this teaches you a different lesson. What would that be and how is it relevant to you in sports and life?

Compassion as Catalyst

*A distinguished Zen master was holding a meditation retreat
of several weeks' duration, with students traveling from all over
Japan to attend. During one of these retreat gatherings, a student
was caught stealing. The theft was reported to the master with a
demand for the offender to be thrown out; but the wise teacher
ignored the matter.*

*Later, the same student was caught stealing again, and
once more the Zen teacher disregarded the complaint. The other
students became very angry at this refusal and drew up a petition
demanding that the thief be dismissed, or else all the other students
would leave in protest.*

*When the master had read their petition, he called them all
before him. "You are all wise brothers," the teacher told them. "You
know the difference between what is right and what is not right.
You may leave and go somewhere else to study if you wish, but this
poor brother doesn't even know right from wrong. If I don't teach
him, who will? I am going to keep him here even if every one of
you leave."*

*A flood of tears fell like a waterfall down the face of the
brother who had taken their things. He had lost all desire to ever
steal again.*

Here is a lesson about humility, compassion, human kindness, and respect. How can you use this lesson in sports and life to help others stay on the right path?

There are other ways to look at this. How could you see it differently?

Attend to Your Side of the Street

When a Zen teacher returned to Japan after many years of diligent spiritual study, many desired to interview him and to ask him obscure questions. But when this learned master received visitors, which was not at all a frequent happening, he rarely answered their questions.

One day, a fifty-year-old Zen student said to the master, "I have studied the teachings of Zen since I was a small child, but the traditions say one thing that I cannot understand. It is said that even the grass and trees will become enlightened. This seems very strange to me."

"What use is it to talk of how grass and trees become enlightened?" asked the teacher. "The question at hand is how you yourself can become enlightened. Did you ever think of that?"

"I never thought of it that way," confessed the old man.

"Then go home and think it over, and take care of your own side of the street," finished the Zen master.

Rather than be concerned about how others are advancing, focus instead on yourself and how you are moving forward in your sports and life.

How and why is this relevant to you? Do you see some other lesson to be learned from this story?

 The Competitive Buddha

Miso for Everyone

A monk who was a cook at a Zen monastery decided to take extra good care of his old teacher's health by feeding him only the freshest miso, a fermented paste of soybeans mixed with wheat and yeast. The master, upon noticing that he was being served better miso than his students, asked, "Who is the cook today?"

The cook was sent for and appeared before the teacher; upon inquiring, the teacher found out that the cook believed that with the master's advanced age and high position, he was only supposed to eat the freshest miso. The old teacher told the cook, "So then you think I shouldn't eat at all." At that, he went into his room, locking the door behind him.

The cook sat outside the master's door, asking his pardon, for hours, then days, but the old teacher refused to answer for seven days.

At last,, a disheartened disciple yelled to the master: "You may be all right, old teacher, but this young monk here needs to eat. He cannot go without food forever!"

Hearing this, the teacher opened the door with a smile. He told the cook, "I insist upon eating the same food as the least of my followers. Do not forget this when you become the teacher."

Lesson being, regardless of rank or stature in life, we are all human beings and must be treated equally, and it's important to remember that when you're in charge. Why and how is this relevant to you in sports and life?

What might be an even better interpretation for you, and how is that relevant to your life at this point?

The Transformative Tunnel

Once a samurai's son came to the capital city to make his fortune; there he entered the service of a high official as part of his retinue. But the young man fell for the official's wife; she returned his feelings, but their affair was soon discovered. In self-defense, the young man slew the official before running away with his wife.

Both of them eventually came to be thieves. But the woman was so greedy that the young man fell out of love with her. At last, he left her and made a journey to a faraway province, where he lived the life of a wandering beggar.

To atone for his past, the young man committed himself to accomplishing a major good deed. He became aware that there was a terribly hazardous road winding over a cliff that had caused many people to die or suffer crippling injuries, and seeing an opportunity to alleviate others' suffering, he resolved to dig a tunnel right through the mountain.

While he spent his days begging for food, at night, he was hard at work digging his tunnel. When thirty years had passed, the tunnel was almost half a mile long, 20 feet high, and 30 feet wide.

But two years before the tunnel was finished, the son of the official he had killed, who was a highly skilled swordsman, found out where the young man was and came to kill him to avenge his father's murder.

"I am willing to give you my life with no argument," said the young man. "But please, first help me finish this work. As soon as it is finished, on that day you may kill me."

So the son of the official waited for the day when the tunnel would be done. A number of months passed while the young man kept on digging. The son grew tired of just hanging around doing nothing while he waited, and he began to help with the digging.

After helping with the work for more than a year, he began to admire the young man's determination and character.

Finally, the tunnel was complete and people could now use it and therefore travel safely.

"Now cut off my head," the man told the official's son. "My task is complete."

"How can I cut off my own teacher's head?" asked the younger man with tears in his eyes.

Although we all make mistakes and end up doing the wrong thing and hurting others, if you atone for your past and do good deeds, you'll be admired for your true intention and character. Why and how is this relevant to you in sports and life?

You may learn another lesson from this story. How could that help you in sports and life?

The Power of Belief

A great Japanese warrior decided to attack the enemy even though he was vastly outnumbered, since he only had one-tenth as many fighting men as the opposition commanded. He knew he would win, but his men were in doubt.

On the way, he stopped at a Shinto shrine, telling his soldiers, "After I pay my respects at the shrine, I'll flip a coin. If it's heads, we'll win; if it's tails, we will lose. Destiny holds our fate in her hand."

The warrior leader went into the shrine and remained there a while, offering silent prayers. Then when he came forth, he tossed a coin; it came up heads. Seeing this, his soldiers were so eager for battle that they won easily.

"No one can change the hand of destiny," his retainer told him after the victory.

"Indeed not," said the warrior, showing his man the coin, on which both sides showed heads either way.

> The lesson here could be: Whether you believe you can or believe you can't, you're probably right. It's all about the power of belief. Why and how is this important to you in sports and life?
>
> How else can you interpret this passage, and how can that help you now?

Killing Life, Killing Time

A Zen master gave his disciples a teaching one day: "Those who speak out against killing and who wish to spare the lives of all conscious beings are right. It is right to protect even animals and insects. But what about people who kill time, what about those who destroy wealth, and what of those who destroy political economy? They should not be overlooked. Beyond that, what about those who preach without having experienced enlightenment? Such a person is killing Buddhism."

The lesson here is about the importance of integrity in all aspects of life. It is wrong to kill no matter what that relates to, whether it's the life of a sentient being or the life of a day. How might this be relevant in your sports and life?

What other lesson might this story teach and why, and how is that important to you?

The Thought and the Stone

A Chinese Zen teacher known for wisdom lived alone in a small temple in the country. One day, four traveling monks showed up, asking if they might build a fire to warm themselves in his yard.

While they were fetching the firewood and making it ready, the teacher heard them having a debate on the topic of subjectivity and objectivity. Joining them, the teacher said, "See that large stone over there. Do you consider it to be inside or outside your mind?"

One of the monks responded, "From the Buddhist point of view, everything is an objectification of the mind, so I would think that the stone is inside my mind."

"Your head must feel quite heavy," observed the teacher, "if you are carrying around a stone like that in your mind."

Our thoughts dictate how we feel. They have an energy of their own and affect how we feel, behave, and perform. Why and how is this relevant to performance in sports and life?

Could there be another interpretation of this story? If so, how is it relevant to you?

The Competitive Buddha

Detaching and Letting Go

The disciple of an aged Zen master was sitting at his teacher's bedside during the last days before his passing. His teacher had already chosen him as his successor.

A temple had recently burned down, and the disciple had been busy rebuilding the structure. The teacher asked him, "What are you going to do when you finish getting the temple rebuilt?"

"When you recover from this sickness, we want you to speak there," said the disciple.

"But what if I do not live until then?"

"Then we will find someone else," replied the student.

"But what if you cannot find anyone?" the master went on.

His student answered loudly: "Don't ask such foolish questions. Just go to sleep."

The lesson here is about the futility of worry and to let go of what you cannot control, like future outcomes. Why and how is this important to our experience of sports and life?

What else does this story bring up for you?

Impermanence

There was a Zen master who had been very clever even as a young boy. His teacher possessed a valuable and rare antique teacup. One day, the boy happened to break the cup; he was bewildered and very unsure of what to do next. As he heard the footsteps of his old teacher approaching, he hid the pieces of the cup by holding them behind his back. When his master came in, the boy asked him, "Why do people have to die?"

"It is natural," explained the older man. "Everything must one day die and has only so long to live."

His student, showing his master the pieces of the shattered cup, proclaimed, "It was your cup's time to die."

The lesson here is profound. It is about the concept of the impermanence of all things. Why and how is this relevant to your sports and life?

Do you believe that everything must end? How is this relevant to you?

Go Slower, Arrive Sooner

Once there was a young man who was the son of a famous swordsman.

But his father disowned him in the belief that his son's ability was never going to be good enough to qualify him to become a master of the sword.

So the young man journeyed to a mountain where a famous swordsman lived to discover the truth of the matter. But the renowned swordsman only confirmed his father's judgment, telling him, "You desire to learn the art of the sword under my tutelage? You will not be able to fulfill the requirements."

"But if I work hard at it, how long will it take me to become a master?" the persistent young man asked.

"The rest of your life," the swordsman told him.

"I cannot wait that long. I am willing to endure any hardship if you will only take me on as your student. If I agree to be your devoted servant, then how long might it take?"

"Oh, maybe ten years," the swordsman relented.

"My father is getting on in years, so I will have to take care of him before long," the young man went on. "If I work more intensively, how long would it take me to master the sword?"

"Oh, maybe thirty years," said the swordsman.

"Why is that?" cried the young man. "First you said ten years, and now you tell me thirty years. I am willing to endure any hardship to master this art in the shortest time!"

"Well, in that case, you will have to stay with me and study for seventy years. A man in as much of a hurry as you are to get results rarely learns quickly."

"Very well," the young man declared, finally understanding that he was being admonished for his impatience, "I agree."

This is a classic story in the Zen tradition about impatience. When you try to force things or make them happen on a specific timetable, it frequently causes delay because attempting to hurry things causes tension and stress, making it take longer. The Buddha says, go slower, arrive sooner. Why and how is this relevant in your sports and life?

Is there a deeper message here? If so, what might that be?

Storytelling Zen

There was once a famous storyteller whose listeners found his love stories moving; and when he told them a war story, his listeners felt as if they themselves were present on the field of battle.

One day, the storyteller met a layman who had nearly embraced mastery in Zen; the man requested a story, saying, "I understand that you are the best storyteller in our land and that you have the ability to make people laugh or cry whenever you choose. Tell me my favorite story, the one about the Peach Boy. When I was a small child, I used to sleep next to my mother, who often would tell me this legend. By the time she reached the middle of the story, I would fall fast asleep. Tell me the story just as my mother used to do."

The famous storyteller did not dare even attempt to do this. He asked for time to study the tale. Several months later, he returned to the layman and asked him, "Please give me a chance to tell you the story."

"Some other day," the man answered.

The storyteller was sharply disappointed. He studied some more and returned to try again. The layman turned him down many times. Whenever the storyteller would start to talk, the man would stop him, saying, "You are not yet telling it like my mother."

It took the storyteller five years to be able to tell the legendary tale as the layman's mother had told it to him.

Thus, the layman imparted Zen to the renowned storyteller.

The lesson here is about persistence, faith, and perseverance. To do things well, you must diligently practice and know that it can take much time and frustration to reach mastery.

Why and how this is relevant is quite obvious, don't you think?

Midnight Rambler

Many pupils were studying meditation under a wise Zen master. One of them used to get up in the middle of the night, scale the temple wall, and go into the nearby town on a pleasure trip.

Upon inspecting the dormitories one night, the master discovered his student was not in his bed and then found the high stool he had used to help him climb over the wall. The master removed the stool and instead stood there in its place.

When the roving student returned, with no idea that his teacher was standing in place of the stool, he put his feet on top his master's head and jumped down to the ground. Once the wanderer understood what he had just done, however, he was horrified.

The master said only, "It is quite chilly in the early morning. Do be careful not to catch a cold."

The pupil never wandered out at night again.

> Do the right thing, even when you think no one is watching, because at some point, your behavior will be discovered.
>
> Why and how is this relevant to sports and life?

Keep the Lantern Lit

In Japan in earlier times, lanterns made of bamboo and paper with candles inside were common. One night, a blind man was offered a lantern to carry home with him by a friend he was visiting.

"I have no need of a lantern," he said. "Dark or light, it is all the same to me."

"I know a lantern will not help you find your way," his friend replied, "but if you don't carry a lantern, someone else may bump into you. So please take it."

The blind man started off walking with the lantern, but before he had walked very far, someone ran into him rather hard. "Look where you are going!" he admonished the stranger. "Can't you see the light of this lantern?"

"Your candle has burned out, brother," the stranger replied.

You may feel secure in what you know and what you can do, but it is equally important to be prepared when others are not. Be aware of all that surrounds you in the present moment. How and why is this relevant to your sports and life?

How can this story be interpreted in a way that suits you best?

EPILOGUE

From Little Streams Come Big Rivers

"Living in accordance with natural hierarchy is not a matter
of following a series of rigid rules or structuring your days
with lifeless commandments. The world has order and power
and richness that can teach you how to conduct your life
artfully with kindness to others and care for yourself."

—Chogyam Trungpa, Tibetan Buddhist scholar and author

In the insightful words of Chogyam Trungpa, the world does
have an order of its own, the laws implicit in its created order.
Simply put, natural law is the way things are. When the Buddha
eats a lot, the Buddha gets fat—unless he eats the right food
and exercises. This is what happens…it's the way it is, naturally.
You don't have to be a physicist to understand the law of
gravity: What goes up must go down. And as is implied in the
opening quote, natural law and Buddhism are a marriage made
in heaven. Throughout this book, you have been soaking in the
continual dance between the Buddha and these natural laws,
which are integral to what liberates you from suffering as you
walk the path of mastery. Living, playing, and competing in
harmony with such precepts leads to levels of peace, joy, and
happiness rarely achieved.

Let's begin with this provocative thought: "Little Streams
Make Big Rivers." This is the way of nature. You can count on
it. Running to the top of Mount Evans in Colorado, which is
over 14,000 feet in height, I witnessed the little rivulets created

by the runoff of snowmelt during spring and early summer. These formed thousands of little creeks, all converging to form many streams that emptied into a tiny river. Fed by many streams, over millennia, this river grew larger and more powerful as it carved a path forming the Grand Canyon; that raging river is called the mighty Colorado River. Here's my interpretation: Notice how in life, all the big happenings and results and outcomes always require many, many small interconnected circumstances, which create enormous opportunities when they converge. If you pay attention and notice the process of life, that's the way it is, in accordance with natural law.

So it is with the journey of *The Competitive Buddha*. The convergence of all of these Buddhist teachings, natural law. and lived truths with the world of athletes enables all of us to live, play, and compete in a place called mastery. These so-called laws are not ideas to dogmatize or debate. They simply exist, like it or not. We either suffer or not depending on the choices we make with what nature offers us. When you align with natural law, you have access to an enormous power or potential that is always available when you are mindful of it. Life can be quite fulfilling when we act and behave accordingly. Trying to fight, resist, or control these natural patterns produces a life of suffering and struggle is what Buddhist thought tells us.

For example, rubbing your hand vigorously against the grain on a slab of unsanded redwood could ruin your afternoon. Slicing turkey breast against the grain creates an aesthetic disaster. Fighting ocean currents can be exhausting and futile. As a matter of fact, nature demands that you go with the flow in anything you encounter; if we fail to act accordingly, problems ensue. Here are few more examples to serve as reference points to facilitate your awareness of how nature works:

- Errors, mistakes, setbacks and failures cannot be avoided. They are teachers helping us to grow, expand, and learn.

- Change is constant; nothing remains the same. Life is up and down, sad and happy, fluidity and stiffness in turn.

- Karma is real. What goes around, comes around.

- Aging is a natural process, with each stage giving you an opportunity for growth.

- Happiness is ephemeral. It comes and goes.

- Letting go and detachment are essential to happiness. When a person does not cultivate awareness of when letting go is necessary and act on it, the result is suffering.

- Impermanence is real. Like it or not, nothing lasts forever.

- Patience, humility, gratitude, and faith are virtues in harmony with natural law that make the journey easier.

Resistance to these Buddha laws creates much of our struggle in sports and life. What I am suggesting is that you flow with the way things are meant to be. Observe what happens to a pine tree during a huge snowstorm. The branches fill with snow and are susceptible to cracking because they remain rigid, whereas a willow tree branch will bend when weighted by snow and release the heavy load, bouncing back to its original position unharmed.

Observe a young child and an adult skiing down a hill. Notice how each handles a fall—the child rolls with the direction of force, while more often than not an adult will stiffen, desperately trying to resist the inevitable. The child then laughs, gets up, and continues down the slope; the adult waits for a stretcher.

To bring harmony and joy to your life, consider all the competitive Buddha lessons within this book and how they work. Begin to listen to the way of nature. Observing and obeying nature's laws teaches you to develop unlimited personal power. There are no mistakes on this path, just lessons. You will no longer try to put a round peg into a square hole. Without effort, the square hole welcomes the square peg.

Eventually, if you begin to move in harmony with nature, with the way natural law works, all things will work out in a way that is appropriate for your life, regardless of what you may think about the outcome. (This is true even though it may not seem right at the time—outcomes can be strange.) Often, you will have the "Ahah experience" at some point in the future: "*Ahah!* That's what was happening. That had to happen this way because of this." It couldn't have come out better even if you had tried to force things and pushed for what you thought was the "right" way. Things work out! Accepting the laws of nature, trusting our perceptions of the world, relying on our instincts and intuition, balancing our extremes, and harmonizing with the flow will all contribute to feelings of personal freedom, security, self-reliance, self-acceptance, and personal power. These are the essential ingredients that can enable you to experience true abundance and fulfillment in your life as an athlete, coach, leader, parent, and mentor.

The basic message of this book is that performance mastery and leadership in sports as well as all of life is a deep, mindful, inner spiritual journey. When you see the connections between the teachings of the competitive Buddha and the laws of nature, good things happen. Suffering is minimized and peace, joy, happiness, and mastery proliferate. That's not my opinion, it's what I observe to be a result of natural law, principles of essential order and power that help you to conduct your life beautifully with harmony and balance.

This internal journey is not a straight-line path up and forward. It is a circular adventure complete with moments of bliss only to be followed by moments of pain and suffering. The key is to use all the strategies, tools, and ways to get back on the path of mastery you've learned in this book. Life is a dance, one moment smooth, fluid, and flowing, yet in the next becoming wild, crazy, spastic, and flailing all over the place. These natural Buddha laws will get you back on track.

Think of going rafting down the Colorado River, and you'll get a clear picture of what happens when you launch on this journey. It changes direction and at times seems to be going back to the start. The pace quickens rapidly through the narrows yet dramatically slows as the river widens. Sometimes the water is clear, other times it is murky and cloudy; exhilarating yet placid; raging yet calm. If you try to slow down when it speeds up, you struggle; if you speed up when it slows down, you will encounter resistance. You can't push the river. Paddle upstream and frustration will take over. You can choose to end the trip at any time, but you will do so at your own risk. The most exuberant journey is to give yourself over to the power of the river, for if you do, you will experience wonderful inner joy and the fulfillment of life as it is meant to be. If you could see the river's path (your inner journey) from a higher perspective, you would see clearly that there is a natural progression and flow. And like the river, *The Competitive Buddha* way in this book is a journey with ups and downs, turns and surprises, cloudy and clear times. Let it flow! You need to trust—it's a must if you are to compete, play, and live masterfully.

I will conclude this book with these thoughts for you on your journey. Choose the competitive Buddha approach for your work, and commit yourself to it with all your heart. When you commit, you will experience profound wisdom and inspiration for all of sports and life. While reflecting on his own athletic path, scholar and mythologist Joseph Campbell recalled in his book *The Hero's Journey* that the years in his life when he was a world-class athlete at Columbia University were a beautiful period. "I think that meant more to me than anything else, my running on the track. I learned more about living from that time than any other time in my life." The journey of the competitive Buddha *is* the archetypal hero's journey, and along the way, something extraordinary happens when you align with this Buddha way. You begin to up your game in athletics, business, and life and experience the joy, pleasure, and meaning that you were meant to have. Bon voyage!

NOTABLE BIBLIOGRAPHY

Essential Classics that Advance the Buddha Sports Journey

Here is a compilation of twenty-four books in a bibliography with an annotated format, books that speak to the relationship of Buddhist thought to performance in sports and life. I include this section hoping that you, the reader, have been so inspired by what you've read thus far that you'd like to advance your learning on the masterful path of the competitive Buddha. I used all of these books and more in one way or another to enhance and shed light on the lessons I've learned in the trenches while bringing the teachings of the Buddha to thousands of athletes in my forty-year career.

While most of these texts reference a connection between Eastern thought and athletics in some fashion, others serve as primers and an entryway into the philosophy of Buddhism, giving you a base or foundation for this new perspective in your life.

In no way do I intend this to be an exhaustive, thorough, probing and comprehensive collection of all Buddhist wisdom; I simply want to expose you to others who are aligned with my work and can be helpful to you in advancing your journey when you're ready to go forward.

This is a never-ending competitive Buddha journey, and neither you nor I ever need be without a book to keep us company on the way and nudge us joyfully along.

The Mindful Athlete
by George Mumford

In this simple yet profound book, Mumford shares the Buddhist techniques and strategies he's used throughout his career, which has included working with Phil Jackson's Bulls and Lakers, Olympians, collegiate athletes, and corporate executives. This is a groundbreaking approach that can transform the performance of anyone looking to elevate their game.

Zen Mind, Beginner's Mind
by Shunryu Suzuki

This is one of the great modern spiritual classics, one widely considered the best first book to read on Zen Buddhism. Suzuki presents the basics in a way that is remarkably clear and succinct. For example, he states, "In the beginner's mind, there are many possibilities, but in the expert's, there are few." Seldom have so few words provided teachings as rich as these.

Sacred Hoops
by Phil Jackson

Sacred Hoops is an inside look at the higher wisdom of teamwork from coach Phil Jackson. At the heart of the book is Jackson's philosophy of mindful basketball. This book will show how this iconic coach has developed a way of leadership based on Eastern thought, emphasizing the Buddhist truths about awareness, compassion, and selflessness. This inspiring book is for anyone interested in the human spirit. It is an insightful and masterful blend of ageless wisdom applied to sports and life.

Tiger Virtues
by Alex Tresniowski

Based on Buddhist principles, *Tiger Virtues* shares legendary golf athlete Tiger Woods' approach and how he has used his Buddhist upbringing to maximize his ability. The book explains how every one of us can follow the Tiger Way and position ourselves to master our sport and experience transcendence. These eighteen virtues will inspire and empower you to approach the degree of spiritual focus of Tiger Woods by incorporating these Buddha lessons into your game and life.

Golf's Three Noble Truths
by James Ragonnet

In this enlightening and practical book, James Ragonnet applies the classic teachings of the Buddha to golf using the core three Buddhist values of Awareness, Balance, and Unity. Entertaining brief essays and stories demonstrate how all golfers (and athletes in any sport) regardless of background or skill level can use these transformative qualities to experience their full human potential. Not only will you improve your performance in sports, you will improve your life as you become a better version of yourself as a person. Here is another amazing book on the growing list of how the Buddha can inspire, empower, and encourage a higher level of overall functioning in life.

Thinking Body, Dancing Mind
by Jerry Lynch and Al Huang

In this classic bestseller, Lynch and Huang teach you the time-honored principles of masterful performance in not only athletics, but all competitive arenas of life, using Taoist strategies to unlock the extraordinary powers of body, mind, and spirit. The authors encourage you to let go of obsession with winning in order to experience victory; to find the courage to risk failure in order to realize your full potential; and to see how your vulnerabilities are actually your best strengths. This is a unique, profound, provocative, and practical book, one that is simple yet brilliant.

Buddha's Brain
by Rick Hansen

Here is a powerful account of the intersection of Buddhist thought and neuroscience that unfolds how to change your brain to change your world. By combining neuroscience breakthroughs with insights from thousands of years of contemplative Buddhist practice, this book will help you to begin to use your mind to shape your life for greater happiness, wisdom, and heightened performance through a greater sense of inner confidence. This clear, easy-to-read work is filled with practical tools and skills to use in daily life to tap into the unused potential of your brain and rewire it for greater well-being and mastery. Rick Hansen is both a neuropsychologist and teacher of mindful meditation for contemplative wisdom.

The Way of Zen
by Alan Watts

With insight and brilliance, Alan Watts examines the history of Zen Buddhism and shows how this ancient spiritual tradition makes it possible to live freely in today's chaotic and tense world. In this easily readable classic, Watts offers an explanation of how this unique Eastern approach can help you be completely and simply human. An excellent comprehensive work that will familiarize you with the principles and practice of this ancient philosophy.

The Spirited Walker
by Carolyn Scott Kortge

No matter how fast or far you walk, whether on a treadmill or in a forest, alone or with others, this easy-to-use guide will help you along the path of mental and spiritual exercise. This book gives you easy-to-implement exercises, visualizations, and affirmations that transform fitness walking into a meditative practice of spiritual awareness, renewal, and vitality. Practical advice, humor, and stories help motivate you to walk the path, one that puts caring for your soul on equal footing with care of your body. Kortge will show you how the simple act of walking can take you "inward bound" to places you never knew existed as you celebrate being fully alive.

At Home in the World
by Thich Nhat Hanh

Written by the world's most revered master of mindfulness, this thought-provoking and inspiring work is a collection of autobiographical stories from the life of this Zen master and peace activist. Thich Nhat Hanh uses storytelling to share valuable and important insights taken from his own rich and remarkable life and the lives of others. How he chooses to live his life, is the essence of his teaching; his life is his message, and it's all within this remarkable book.

Why Buddhism Is True
by Robert Wright

In this New York Times bestseller, Robert Wright tells us everything we need to know about the science, philosophy, practice, and power of Buddhism. At the core of Buddhism is the simple claim that we suffer because we don't see the world clearly. Wright shows how meditation can help relieve suffering, loosen the grip of anxiety, regret, and hatred, and deepen your appreciation of beauty and other people. Drawing on the latest in neuroscience and psychology, he explains why this path of truth and the path of happiness are identical. To which I add, having read this profound book, that they are also parallel to the path of sports performance.

The Way of Aikido
by George Leonard

In this classic book, Leonard shares the secrets of this Eastern philosophy that is also the most demanding and radical of all martial arts. He demonstrates how aikido can be applied to daily life, including performance in all sports as well, to help set you on the path of composure, harmony, and spiritual centeredness. Enlightening and replete with deep wisdom, the text describes ways in which this martial art can provide you with the power to transform your performance in sports and life by connecting you to the essential natural laws of the planet. Another of his dozen books, *Mastery: Keys to Success & Long-Term Fulfillment*, is also a brilliant bestseller that is aligned with the Buddha Sports way.

Chop Wood, Carry Water
by Rick Fields and others

Fields presents us with a guide whose contents are easily applied to your sports world. It is filled with advice, hints, stories, encouragement, warnings, and cautions for your sports journey as you live it throughout your life. This book contains an abundance of Buddhist wisdom that can be integrated into your modern living, including work, play, competition, and relationships—illuminating the quest for spiritual fulfillment and extraordinary performance, whether athletically or in other arenas of life. This book answers the deeper question of how can we apply the wisdom and insights of the great spiritual traditions to the way we live, develop, and perform.

Zen Golf
by Joseph Parent

Author Joseph Parent, a noted PGA tour coach and a respected Buddhist teacher, draws on this natural connection to teach athletes in golf and all sports how to compete with more consistency and less stress and frustration, achieving mastery in the process. By applying classic insights and stories from the Buddhist tradition, he shows how to make one's mind an ally, cultivate calm, and clear the mental fog that leads to poor shots, helping to eliminate bad habits and mistakes. Though the Buddhist wisdom in this book is expressed through the game of golf, it is applicable to all games in sport. This is one of my go-to books on this list, a definite favorite when I want a quick yet effective spiritual sports fix.

The Inner Game of Tennis
by Timothy Gallwey

This is the classic of all classics when it comes to the mental game of sports using unconventional methods as guides to the consciousness side of peak performance. Reading this awesome work, you will come to value the art of relaxed focus above all other skills and learn that the secret to victory lies in the effortlessness of effort—in not trying too hard. Gallwey teaches that when the mind is calm and at one with the body, you will begin to surpass self-imposed limits and uncover the will to perform well. This book will help you to rely more on your unconscious mind and your strong intuitive sense. Put this book on your bucket list of books to read. These principles lie at the very foundation of the competitive Buddha way.

Let Them Play
by Jerry Lynch

Here is a book that combines psychological insight with spiritual principles from Buddhism to catalyze sports parents mindfully inspire and empower their young stars to have more joy, fun, and success not just in sports, but in all of life. This profound book gives parents specific strategies and tools to help kids perform in the zone of mastery as well as an entire section addressing a useful code of conduct for parents attending their child's sporting events. It is a blueprint for raising happy, healthy athletes for success in sports. Coaches like Steve Kerr, Phil Jackson, Anson Dorrance, and others highly recommend this book on the path to becoming the best sports parent you can be.

The Competitive Buddha

Wherever You Go, There You Are
by Jon Kabat-Zinn

Jon Kabat-Zinn maps out a simple path for cultivating the heart of Buddhism: how to practice mindful meditation in one's life. It addresses both those coming to meditation for the first time and longtime practitioners as well. Here is a remarkably concise, clear, and poignant guide to meditation, one that contains all the necessary instructions to engage in this key practice on your own. Jon's definition of mindfulness, which is also included elsewhere within this book you are holding, is worth repeating here. Mindfulness means paying attention in a particular way: on purpose, in the present moment and nonjudgmentally. This book will connect your mind and heart, an exquisitely necessary prerequisite for mastery.

Zen in the Martial Arts
by Joe Hyams

In this classic, Hyams reveals to you how the daily application of Zen principles not only helped him develop his physical expertise but gave him the mental and spiritual discipline to make positive changes in how he handled self-image, work pressure, and competition in sport. He demonstrates how mastering the spiritual Buddha aspects in martial arts can dramatically alter the quality of life and your ability to reach your performance goals, helping you make total use of your full human capacity. Learn how to apply the principles of Zen to sport for inner strength you never knew you had.

Golf in the Kingdom
by Michael Murphy

Michael Murphy has written a book that is considered the go-to work on the deeper mysteries of golf, a gospel for those who know or suspect that golf (and all sports) is more than merely a game to pass time. This vivid account reveals the possibilities for transformation that reside in the human soul. The *San Francisco Chronicle* calls it "a masterpiece on the mysticism of golf." There is much in this brilliant book that can be used in all sports as well as in the journey of life.

Spirit of the Dancing Warrior
by Jerry Lynch and Chungliang Al Huang

This work leans heavily on the ancient wisdom of Buddhism and Taoism to help you become more spiritually awake through sports and fitness. It is a joyful companion as you navigate the challenging path of sports and spirituality, from the ordinary to the extraordinary. This book will help you develop stronger, more meaningful relationships with your sports, yourself, and your life using practical and insightful gems and soulful nuggets. You will learn to shift from focusing on the external battlefields to an interior landscape of overcoming fear, failure, and self-doubt. These battles are won with core values called 'weapons of the heart.'

Win the Day
by Jerry Lynch

In this seminal book, Dr. Jerry Lynch outlines the bulk of his work with 115 championship teams over a thirty-year span using the values and virtues of Buddhism, Taoism, and Native American traditions to help coaches and athletes learn how

The Competitive Buddha

to connect, care, and love each other while at the same time helping to create, cultivate, drive, and sustain a team culture of performance mastery. He makes available practical, easy-to-implement tools, strategies, lessons, exercises, and stories that help strengthen your internal North Star while building a championship culture with your team.

Eleven Rings: The Soul of Success
by Phil Jackson and Hugh Delehanty

The is a memoir of legendary coach Phil Jackson's eleven NBA championships, one filled with candid insights into the alchemy of leadership. He explores everything from psychology and Native American traditions to Buddhist meditation; and in the process, he offers a leadership approach based on authenticity and selfless teamwork in the world of professional competitive sports. He reveals how he learned the secrets of mindfulness and team cohesion and has applied them to success on the court. Jackson was tagged by the media as the "Zen Master" who led by awakening athletes' better angels rather than playing to their egos and fear. This book includes many of the competitive Buddha concepts as they relate to sports and life.

Every Moment Matters
by John O'Sullivan

How do the world's most successful coaches get the best from their athletes? How do top coaches design practices, inspire their players, and build teams that sustain their excellence season after season? How do they instill high-performing behaviors? Do they coach men and women differently? What about coaching their own children? Most importantly, are these secrets available to the rest of us coaching youth, high school, and college teams? In *Every Moment Matters*, renowned coach educator and professional colleague John O'Sullivan brings together hundreds of interviews with top coaches, sport scientists, psychologists, and athletes, distilling them into a blueprint for becoming a more effective and inspiring leader. Great coaches realize something that others do not: *Every moment matters!* You must be intentional about everything you do. Whether you are coaching your local youth soccer team, leading your high school football program, or competing for an NCAA championship, *Every Moment Matters* will give you the tools and strategies to become the coach you always wished you had—and the coach today's athletes crave. It will come as no surprise that John's work draws on the elements of Eastern thought we use in our partnership teaching and our approach to sports.

Embrace Tiger, Return to Mountain
by Chungliang Al Huang

First published in 1973, this all-time classic of Tai Ji literature remains as fresh and illuminating today as when it was first published. Written with true passion and eloquence, this iconic book richly conveys the subtle yet profound philosophy underlying Tai Ji. Movement, stillness, joyfulness, and the ability to live in the present moment are the threads running through the text, as well as the humor and compassion required to acknowledge the impossibility of human perfection. It includes the original foreword by Alan Watts and photographs by Si Chi Ko, one of China's "National Treasures," and it is illustrated with beautiful calligraphy by the author. This timeless masterpiece is essential reading for anybody interested in Chinese Tao and Buddhist thought as well as the practice of Tai Ji. Al Huang wrote a book with Alan Watts and has also cowritten six books with the author of this book.

Buddha Takes the Mound
by Donald Lopez, PhD

Buddha Takes the Mound presents for the first time *The Baseball Sutra*, where it is revealed that the Buddha invented baseball to teach us deep truths about the world and about ourselves. The Buddha shows us how the most profound teachings of Buddhism manifest themselves on the field of play. At the conclusion of the sutra, the Buddha offers meditation instructions for both players and fans, practices that transform our understanding of the game, as we are transformed in the process. Don Lopez offers us yet another work based in scholarship tying together the connection of the Buddha to sports.

PRACTICING GRATITUDE

To my literary agent, Bill Gladstone, who, within an hour of receiving my manuscript, replied, "This is good timing for this book, I have a good instinct that this book will be successful. I can sell this." And sell he did to this awesome publisher, Mango. I am grateful for your enthusiastic support of my work over the years and your belief in me and what I do.

To my associate publisher, Brenda Knight, who knew from the moment she held this book that it would be a project she'd love to direct. Brenda is the quintessential "Truth Teller," making candid, astute, brilliant, and tough suggestions, many of which I was hoping to not hear, yet knew the book was better off because of her input. I am grateful for her and all that I have learned.

To my editorial assistant, Robin Miller, for her kind, generous contribution of "filling the cracks in the concrete," and attending to all the important small details that make the book whole.

To the design director at Mango, Roberto Nunez, who took the book's universal message and translated it into a cover design that sums up the meaning and purpose of this work using the Buddhist and simple-yet-profound ENSO image, a circle that captures all that is within these pages.

To my life partner, Jan, for her continued support of who I am and what I do. She wasn't simply the image of a faithful, patient spouse in the background, tiptoeing through the house, taking care of the chores, and extending an ineffable aura of praise and support. But she did nudge and push a bit when

I needed it most and she still expected me to do all my work around the house, especially my cooking her good meals after her robust patient load as a doctor. She is the competitive Buddha in so many ways. I will love you forever.

To Sally Vaughn, my office assistant without whom there would be complete chaos in getting my writing ready for publication. Her formatting and typing suggestions are a huge help and without her, where would I be? It's so cool that she actually loves what I write.

To all the luminaries who have endorsed my work and sincerely believe that I am making a difference in the lives of others. You've made an enormous difference in my life and I am honored and humbled by your never-ending support.

ABOUT THE AUTHOR

 Jerry first learned about extraordinary performance and excellence as a nationally ranked competitive athlete sponsored by Nike, running world class times from 5,000 meters to the marathon, setting an American record in the half-marathon, and winning a National Championship and many other races against athletes half his age. He took what he learned about himself and life from his competitive days and parlayed it into a dynamic successful career helping athletes and coaches in all sports to use his Buddha performance and leadership strategies to up their game and discover the best version of themselves. His most recent book, *The Competitive Buddha,* is emblematic of his journey of excellence and will serve as a guide for anyone who wishes to join the journey.

To give a clearer sense about his professional life as an author, leader, coach, and mentor, Jerry combines Eastern thought, Native American tradition, and Western psychology to help create mental strength, spiritual dexterity, inspiration, and empowerment, not only for competitive events but for self-awareness, confidence, and how to be the best version of yourself each day.

Dr. Lynch has been recognized as one of the top five in his profession nationwide. He has worked with teams, coaches, and athletes in the NBA, Pro Lacrosse, Major League Soccer, with men's and women's basketball, lacrosse, soccer, tennis, golf, and other sports at the universities of North

Carolina, Duke, Maryland, California, Syracuse, Stanford, Harvard, and Middlebury. In the past thirty years alone, he has help guide 115 championship teams, 55 Final Fours resulting in 39 National Championships at the collegiate and professional levels.

Jerry is a dynamic, entertaining, inspirational, provocative, and humorous teacher and speaker with topics on leadership, coaching, team culture building, winning the relationship game, and core value development.

Some of his presentations include Keynote Talks at the New Zealand National Academy of Sport, Der Deutsche Schmerztog in Germany, the U.S. National Field Hockey Coaches convention, the Ironman Sports Medicine Conference in Hawaii, the USA Lacrosse National Convention, and the NIKE/China Leadership Summit in Lanai, Hawaii.

Dr. Lynch has had extensive media interview coverage with CBS, NBC, and PBS national television, the *New York Times, Oprah Magazine, Sports Illustrated, Baltimore Sun, Outside Magazine* and over four hundred national radio broadcasts, podcasts, and webinars. He cohosts the *Way of Champions* podcast, one of the top rated podcasts in the world for coaches. The author of fourteen books in over ten languages, Dr. Lynch is the founder and director of WAY OF CHAMPIONS, a human potential and performance consulting group helping others master the deeper inner game for sports, business and life.

CONTACT JERRY:

Phone: 831-234-5606
Email: wayofchampions@gmail.com
Website: www.wayofchampions.com

If you would like to set up a speaking engagement, workshop, conference or keynote talk with Dr. Lynch, please contact his office directly via his email address.

Mango Publishing, established in 2014, publishes an eclectic list of books by diverse authors—both new and established voices— on topics ranging from business, personal growth, women's empowerment, LGBTQ studies, health, and spirituality to history, popular culture, time management, decluttering, lifestyle, mental wellness, aging, and sustainable living. We were recently named 2019 *and* 2020's #1 fastest growing independent publisher by *Publishers Weekly.* Our success is driven by our main goal, which is to publish high quality books that will entertain readers as well as make a positive difference in their lives.

Our readers are our most important resource; we value your input, suggestions, and ideas. We'd love to hear from you— after all, we are publishing books for you!

Please stay in touch with us and follow us at:
Facebook: Mango Publishing
Twitter: @MangoPublishing
Instagram: @MangoPublishing
LinkedIn: Mango Publishing
Pinterest: Mango Publishing
Newsletter: mangopublishinggroup.com/newsletter

Join us on Mango's journey to reinvent publishing, one book at a time.